# Scripting Identity

## Writing Cultural Experience

Theresa Carilli

UNIVERSITY PRESS OF AMERICA,® INC.
*Lanham • Boulder • New York • Toronto • Plymouth, UK*

**Copyright © 2008 by**
**University Press of America,® Inc.**
4501 Forbes Boulevard
Suite 200
Lanham, Maryland 20706
UPA Acquisitions Department (301) 459-3366

Estover Road
Plymouth PL6 7PY
United Kingdom

Library of Congress Control Number: 2007940281
ISBN-13: 978-0-7618-3929-3 (paperback : alk. paper)
ISBN-10: 0-7618-3929-1 (paperback : alk. paper)

For Jane Campbell, my mentor, life partner,
beacon of light.

You are a magnificent presence.
There never will be enough lives together.

# Contents

# Acknowledgments

It is with deep gratitude that I wish to acknowledge those individuals who so willingly took risks to create the scripts contained in this book: Adrienne Viramontes, Dave Fanno, Jennifer Bianchi, Erin Okamoto Protsman, Ami Kleminski, and William Boggs. Each of you has given me a piece of yourself that I will treasure and treat with respect. This book was intended to honor your work and to provide the opportunity for others to learn from your risk-taking.

Special thanks to Ami Kleminski for her assistance and Jane Campbell for her sharp editorial eye.

## The Great Hartford Circus Fire

I used to believe in tightrope walkers
    In ballet dancers,
    Wild tigers—
    And happiness.

My father holds my hand tightly, firmly.

I feel safe.

I used to believe that clowns had higher powers
And that balloons were magical devices,
Until the devastation ripped through my town—
Taking my father from me.

The canvas burnt to the ground by a frail-minded
young man—
Who spoke to a force that no one could see.

Taking my father—

Away.

Theresa Carilli

# Introduction

Over the last few years, the discipline of Performance Studies has focused on performative ways of being. Such performative ways of being have taken form and shape as autoethnographies (Bochner & Ellis, 1996; Denzin, 2003; Lockford, 2004; Pelias, 1999, 2004). This focus encourages the processing of body epistemology as reflective discourse. The evolution of this focus and turn in Performance Studies has an intriguing history which can be traced to a turn away from Oral Interpretation, a desire to examine the complexities and nuances of various texts, an inquiry into the hegemony of positivism, and a longing for acceptance and recognition in the Communication discipline, which might have otherwise looked upon creative endeavors with disdain. The work of the postmodern ethnographers/critical theorists in the 80's and 90's opened a door for the once-marginalized discipline to play a key role in dialogue about the nature and truth of methodology in the process of unearthing human communication.

In 1987, Ronald Pelias and James VanOosting published a landmark article, "A Paradigm for Performance Studies" that dramatically altered the direction and role of Performance Studies in the Communication discipline. Pelias and VanOosting carved out a methodology by re-examing text, performer, audience, and event. As a humanitarian discipline, this re-examination, which questioned the definition of aesthetic communication, raised serious issues of agency. No longer were Oral Interpretation scholars required to abide by a literary canon which ignored a culture's history and current status. No longer did Oral Interpretation need to rely on stylized methods of elocution and presentation. Instead, the "magical" renaming freed members of the Performance Studies scholarly community to create imaginative texts or to use textual information from various sources, i.e., news clippings, conversation, and nonfiction. By using such texts, this community of scholars became a group of activists and rhetoricians—creating political claims and arguments through the chosen texts.

The work of Kristin Langellier on personal narrative (1989) revolutionized and underscored the rhetorical and political leanings of Performance Studies. Personal narratives extracted from interviews or written as a creative purging quickly became recognized as raw data for the study of human communication. At the same time, ethnographer Victor Turner (1986), Performance Studies scholar Dwight Conquergood (1985) and environmentalist theatre expert Richard Schechner (1985) were dialoguing about the connections between performance and cultural texts, pioneering the field of performative ethnography, the precursor to autoethnography. Through performative ethnography, the researcher could study a culture and embody that culture in performance. By so doing, the researcher would gain bodily awareness of cultural experience while also empathizing with the experience of the other.

Concurrently, ethnographers like Barbara Myeroff (1980), James Clifford (1986), and George Marcus and Michael Fisher (1986) recognized that the "crisis of representation" that caused great strife for anthropologists was making its way into the discussions of representation in all the social sciences, including communication. These ethnographers were heeding the warning issued by Clifford Geertz (1973) that the study of culture was really "the construction of other people's construction of what they and their compatriots are up to" (p. 9). As these and other ethnographers hashed out the details so that cultural members could speak for themselves, a fascination with autobiography (Okeley & Callaway, 1992) as cultural text entered this dialogue. The recognition that autobiography combined with ethnography could produce a methodology that allowed the cultural member to speak reflectively about his or her own experience has led to our current understanding of autoethnography. Carolyn Ellis and Arthur Bochner (2001) have taken this discussion to a new level, examining the autoethnographic components of literature. Questions of agency, however, still remain with this evolving method. Such questions as whose autoethnographies qualify as cultural information, and who has the right to pen an autoethnography about a particular culture, bring us back to the original question of aesthetic communication and the dismissal of the literary canon.

Having witnessed these questions coming full cycle while Performance Studies scholars rely heavily on autoethnographies as records of the performance of being, with this book I propose a new look at the earlier questions of agency, sharing my own critical reflections on my work as a performative writer as well as my experience of working with students who scripted their cultural identity. In Chapter One, I will discuss my evolution as a performative writer, giving examples of some of my own creative work, which has grown out of my own cultural understanding. In Chapter Two, I will explore how my creative work as a performative writer has inspired me in the classroom, teaching students how to script and write their own cultural identities. Chapters Three through Eight are scripts written by students. Each piece is written in a different genre, thus capturing identity in a manner that complements the culture being explored. I hope this book will encourage writers to examine the role of genre and primary narrative as they are woven into the process of script-building.

## Chapter One

# Performative Writing and the Primary Narrative

### FROM PERSONAL NARRATIVE TO PRIMARY NARRATIVE: A PERSONAL/POLITICAL EVOLUTION

I identify as a performative writer, that is, someone who writes creative work that is oral and that comes to life from the printed page. The vast majority of my creative work has been written in the first person. Personal narratives, monologues, and plays demand character embodiment that produce stories told in the first person.

In my early years as a performative writer, I attempted to draw a connection between culture and creativity based on my belief that the performative writer was much like the participant/observer, and thus, much like the ethnographer. To truly embody character, the writer must pay close attention to the sharpest details of the characters' lives—how they move, use language, and conceal their emotions. To do so, the writer must inhabit the bodies of those whom she renders. This transcendent experience requires a deep reverence for those whom the writer creates. I will use a personal narrative from my own experience, or I will create stories and monologues based on the experiences of individuals who have been significant in my life, or I will develop a story or monologue that is created in the imagination based on a knowingness of others.

As a Performance Studies scholar, I have followed the arguments theorized by the performative ethnographers and introduced as part of the "crisis of representation." Embodying others became one way of exploring and explaining cultural experience (Conquergood, 1985; Schechner, 1985; Turner, 1986). By embodying the stories of cultural group members, the performer develops a deep sense of understanding for the culture. Simultaneously, ethnographers like Edward Bruner, (1986) who studied Native American culture, and Barbara Myeroff (1980) who collected stories of Jewish elders, recognized that

1

cultural members telling their own stories should suffice as ethnographic information. In *Ethnography as Narrative,* Bruner (1986) writes "life experience is richer than discourse" (p. 143), a statement which acknowledges the
value of Native American stories. Barbara Myeroff created the video documentary *Number Our Days* based on her work in a southern California elderly Jewish club. Myeroff attended many of the club's functions to capture
her footage for this spirited yet poignant documentary. Both Bruner and
Myeroff deferred to the voices of the culture's members, operating more as
facilitators or conduits of cultural information.

Performance Studies scholar Kristin Langellier's 1989 article, *Personal
Narratives: Perspectives on Theory and Research,* demonstrated a kinship
with ethnographers, backed by a recognition that personal narratives can give
textured, nuanced, and meaningful information to any study of human communication. The Performance Studies community, who had been working
with personal narratives, continued to develop performances based on the-
matically collected narratives. Many of these performances were rhetorically
charged and gave voice to marginalized cultures. Sharon Bebout's work with
coal miner's wives' narratives (1995) or Lori Montalbano-Phelps' (2004)
work with battered women's narratives are two such examples.

During the 1990s, many Performance Studies conference panels show-
cased narratives written by members of the scholarly community. Issues related to the writing, editing, and embodiment of personal narratives were explored at conferences. In 1998, Sheron Daly edited *The Future of
Performance Studies: Visions and Revisions,* which contained an entire section on issues related to the personal narrative. For this book, I wrote an
article entitled, "Verbal Promiscuity or Healing Art?: Writing the Creative/
Performative Personal Narrative," which describes one method of writing a
creative personal narrative:

> To be considered a creative text, a personal narrative should contain the following
> five elements: (1) It should be either a narrative told from the writer's experience
> or from the writer's embodiment of other individual's experiences, (2) It should
> contain unique language which depicts a way of thinking or moving through the
> world, (3) Conflicts which reflect ambiguities should be present throughout the nar-
> rative, (4) A substantial portion of the narrative should contain mundane details
> which reflect universal experience, and (5) Symbols or metaphors should be pres-
> ent which give broader definition to an overall understanding of the text.

As a member of the Performance Studies community, I had written several
personal narratives about my experiences as a lesbian and an Italian American. Here are two examples of personal narratives that address this intersection. Each of these personal narratives has been written by following the

aforementioned model. In each of these narratives, I attempt to demonstrate the feelings of isolation and alienation contained in the intersection of my identities.

## SECRECY

Dona Maria was a large Sicilian woman who talked like a man. She wore a loose-fitting apron over her faded, flowered dresses, which matched her kitchen wallpaper. Often you could see her extraordinary bosoms protruding from the sides of her dresses. She staggered with a limp and laughed while speaking her native Sicilian. She spoke very little English so our exchanges were brief.

When we were children, my father would take my younger sister and me to visit Dona Maria every few weeks. Her son, Montana Jim, who was nicknamed "Montana" because he had a nose the size of the state, had died at a young age. My father, one of Jim's best friends, paid his respect by visiting Montana's mother, Dona Maria. She would greet us with a large all-encompassing kiss and exclaim in Italian to my father about how both my sister and I had grown. Then she'd scurry off to her refrigerator and present my sister and me with large glasses of sour milk, and on special occasions, stale cookies. My younger sister would grimace while drinking some of the milk, and I would grin at her, amused by her foolishness.

After Dona Maria would pour the milk and give us the cookies, she would take my father outside and show him some newly planted bushes. This meant the whole neighborhood would hear her booming discourse, as she flailed her fleshy arms. Left alone, my sister and I would explore Dona Maria's house. We were fascinated by her living room because she had a collection of "artistic statues"—pastel colored statues of men with huge penises, the type of statues you would see in a cheap gag shop. She was unlike so many other Sicilians who proudly sported Catholic icons or imitations of Michelangelo's sculptures. And, she was quite the renegade by not covering her furniture with thick dingy plastic. So began my fascination with Dona Maria's living room. One day while sitting on the living room floor, I noticed several cookies protruding from her couch slip. This didn't surprise me because I can recall the days when my mother would make pasta and leave it all over the beds to dry. So, I assumed this was some Sicilian knowledge of the relationship between dough and air. Later I learned it was a way to keep the cookies fresh. But Dona Maria kept giving me stale cookies. I hated those cookies. I hated the sour milk. And most of all, I hated my father's respect for this caricature of an Italian woman.

So, with my sister watching, I placed that day's worth of stale cookies back underneath Dona Maria's couch. And from this exercise, I learned about secrecy. I couldn't tell Dona Maria to stop giving me stale cookies and sour milk, and I couldn't tell my father to stop bringing me to visit her.

Years later, when I learned that Dona Maria had passed away, I thought of her fondly, even lovingly. I thank her for teaching me about secrecy. Today, I model myself after Dona Maria. She was a large Sicilian woman who talked like a man. She was loud. She was strong. She was herself.

## A RANDOM ACT

What my cousin Carmela and I have in common is absolutely nothing. Kindly, she meets my partner Jane and me in a hotel in Siracusa, Sicily, preparing to take us to my grandparents' hometown, Palazzolo, Acriede, about 40 miles from Siracusa. We have never met—only conversed over the phone—and she tries not to show her surprise and dismay over my body size. I am large and tall, while she is small and thin, and standing alongside one another we look more like a circus act than cousins. But she remains collected and polite, mannered, and very excited to have the opportunity to speak English. For a short period of time, Carmela's family lived in Australia, where she learned English. Now she teaches the English language to junior high school students. I am ashamed of the way English sounds—like the guttural utterances of some pre-historic animal. Silently, I chastise myself for not learning how to speak Italian. Then I excuse my ignorance as a remnant of immigration and assimilation into American culture. But the real reason I do not speak Italian is because I was so ashamed of my ethnicity. Growing up, I kept my distance from individuals of Italian descent, favoring all that was Anglo, from sugar cookies to creative writers. In an effort to relinquish this shame of being Italian American, I have come to visit Sicily with Jane, my Anglo beloved. Like many Americans of Italian descent, I come looking for what has been lost—hidden information, the last days of life there, the hopes that were never realized.

I often joked that my mother was a first wave feminist—keeping her maiden name before it became fashionable to do so. But the reality is that my parents are cousins with the same last name. This reality keeps me up late at night while I attempt to figure out what relation my aunt would have been to me if my parents had not been cousins. And, of course, I am overcome with fear about the medical background. Theories abound that relatives produce children with weaker immune systems. And then, there's the specter of Thalassemia minor. My father carries the alpha trait while my mother carries the beta trait. When I was a teenager, a medical doctor took special interest in my family because my sisters and I carry both the alpha and beta traits. The research was abandoned when the doctor labeled my family "uncooperative." It was a constant battle for the doctors to collect blood samples on a regular basis. My parents had little interest in contributing to modern science.

So here we are, traveling to my grandparents' hometown. Carmela remains calm and friendly. I am terrified of what I will learn. The stories of my grandparents begin to haunt me. According to a legend dictated by my mother, her father, Francesco, was an "illegitimate" son who was supported by his "*puttana*" (whore) mother. He lived in a barn and slept on a pile of hay. Then there's the anarchist uncle who published an underground newspaper, the aunt who was known as the largest woman in the country, and my great-grandparents, who were really Turks. Through Carmela, I speak to my Aunt Teresina, my mother's first cousin and the family historian, firing my questions as though she is part of a criminal investigation. According to her, there is no *puttana,* no Turk, no anarchist. My hopes of learning the truth are diminished. I must listen to the homes and the walkways for my information.

Before I arrived in Sicily, I had the image that many Americans undoubtedly hold—that of towns with unpaved roads, flocks of sheep, unkempt farmers, and large pasta markets. In my mind, Sicily was a quaint country full of friendly simpletons. I didn't expect cars, highways, cities, or a place that was part of the information age.

Jane and I explored history through the ruins in Segesta and Agriegento and admired architecture in Palermo and Siracusa. We traveled around the country with a dictionary, and thanks to the generosity of the Sicilians, managed to communicate. Their warmth was delightfully familiar to me. During the first few days of our stay, we got lost on the west coast while looking for the town of Erice. By accident, we encountered a hotel in nearby Trapani where we decided to stay for a few evenings. Shaken by our travel experience, Jane and I became teary eyed at the hotel restaurant, having been scolded by the waiter that we had missed out on the *primo* course. Looking around the room, I noticed a large woman in a dark brown wool sweater who stared intently at us. Jane and I both assumed this to be a declaration of the Sicilian contempt for our American "lifestyle choice." The woman, who attempted a few words of English as we struggled with our paltry Italian, was asking us if we were sisters—*sorella.* We shook our heads "no," and resumed our meal. Still, she stared at us. Her stare indicated that she was a key figure at this hotel or in this restaurant, a person who demanded respect. As I took a bite of *secondo,* a fresh tuna, the sauce dripped onto my shirt. Immediately, the woman summoned the waiter, who hurried to our table with a bottle of stain remover. Excitedly, he sprayed the stain remover onto my shirt and proceeded to rub out the stain. As he did this, the woman explained to us, with sharp hand gestures, that one must always keep her clothes clean, for one never knows how long she will need that piece of clothing. For all one knows, something could happen that very day that would alter her future. And clean clothes are a must. We immediately became comrades with this woman, who took a special interest in our comings and goings throughout our stay at her hotel.

A few days later, we met Maria Grammatico, whose life was captured in the book, *Bitter Almonds*. She very graciously extended herself to us, treating us to cappuccino and cookies. At her well-reputed Erice pastry shop, Grammatico sold the book that chronicled her experiences of growing up in a nunnery where she learned the art of making pastry. She was pleased to know that I had read the book. The book had been published in English, so few Sicilians knew of her personal history and fame in America.

In each town we visited, someone either gave me a gift or demonstrated hospitality: a love for humanity, a genuine appreciation of people, even strangers. This was such a contrast to being in America where I feel a fool anytime I extend myself. I had myself convinced that I came from a co-dependent ethnic group. In reality, I come from people who have generous spirits expressed through caring mannerisms. If we were lost, we would be physically escorted to our next destination and treated respectfully. If we were stumped by the language, someone would always make the effort to understand us.

As we enter Palazzolo, I am struck by its beauty—the lush green mountains like cut-out paper dolls, highlighting the background. This pretty town feels open and welcoming—kind and self-contained. Aunt Teresina takes me to the homes of each of my grandparents, who lived in close proximity to one another. While walking around the town, she tells me about my great-grandparents. I must admit something here, difficult though it may be. I envisioned a town where people lived in tents and worked in fields. I believed my great-grandparents to be unimaginably poor, passing around the final crust of bread to their children, while they starved. I imagined each torturous day, tending the fields, caring for the animals.

Instead, I learn that one of my great-grandfathers was an architect, having designed a local building for a baron. As Carmela shows us this building, I stare in awe at the work. While the balcony looks like a simple ornamental structure from the distance, when viewed close up, each pillar contains gargoyles with animated expressions of joy. I stand in front of the faces and laugh as though my great-grandfather knew that one day I would be there in front of his design and we would share a private joke. As we walk on, Aunt Teresina points up the steps to a large blue door, the home of my other great-grandfather, Carmello, a "highway man" known for his magnanimity throughout the town. Then she takes me to each of the homes of my grandmothers.

I had never met either of my grandmothers since each died at such a young age, the repercussions of poverty and living in the frigid American East Coast climate. The yellow door of my maternal grandmother Angelina's home and the grey door of my paternal grandmother Sebastiana's home feel comforting—as if only I could open each door, I would be privy to their lives, as if I would know how they spent their time, what they thought, who each of them was, in her own right. I feel as if I could just open the doors, I would walk into the homes and see them, and they would say something to me that would answer my questions, quell my curiosity, make me feel like I had a home. Instead, the doors remain closed and we proceed to the small local Greek theater.

Later that afternoon, Carmela drives us back to her home in Floridia, near Palazollo. There I meet her family, her husband and daughters, her sister, her sister's husband and newborn child, and her mother, Elivra, Teresina's sister. I err by complimenting Carmela on her home only to learn that this particular part of the home is actually Elvira's. I apologize for my ignorance.

That evening, I learn about Elvira's mother, Benedetta, sister to my grandmother. Benedetta lived well into her 80's while my grandmother died at the age of 37. Finally, I summon up the nerve to ask the question I had wanted to ask for so long—really, the only question that matters. Why was my grandmother sent to America, which turned out to be a death sentence, while Benedetta, Carmela's grandmother, remained in Sicily? After ironing out the details in Sicilian, Carmela explains the situation. "Her father," she began, "did not wish to support your grandmother, Angelina. So he sent her to America with her other sister, Maria."

"But why," I question, "did Benedetta get to stay while my grandmother and her younger sister had to leave?" Again the Italian goes back and forth between Carmela and Aunt Teresina.

"Benedetta," Carmela continues, "was left to care for her mother and father." Carmela and I look deep into each other's eyes, understanding the rules of being an Italian woman and the silence surrounding these rules.

Back in the hotel room that night, I lie awake thinking about Carmela. If Benedetta had been sent to America and my grandmother, Angelina, had stayed to care for her parents, perhaps I might have been born in Sicily and Carmela in America. But instead, by the random act of choosing which daughter would care for her parents, my entire family and cultural history had been altered.

I remember the woman in the restaurant—always to be clean and ready in the event of . . . in the event of . . . you never know. One day, your parents might send you to another country. One day, you might remember Sicily as the lovely place from which you came. One day, you might die in a country that is not really yours, and you will have nothing to say about it . . . .

The following year, Aunt Teresina died. I replayed every moment of our journey through Palazollo. I thought about the pride she had in showing off her hometown. I thought about the way people move through various times and spaces, and yet their spirits leave an imprint of that place they call home. I will always cherish my time with her. I am American and Italian and everything in between.

*I am a random act in a country of survivors.*

In the latter part of the 1990s, personal narratives evolved into autoethnographies—autobiographies that captured cultural experience and reflection. Bochner and Ellis' *Composing Ethnography* (1999) contained articles that delved into such topics as the experience of bulimia or the fieldwork experience of studying witches' covens. This book broadened the field of personal narrative by asserting that autobiographical reflections written by a cultural member serve as meaningful cultural data. For many performative writers, performance could be studied through body epistemology, or how the performer experienced an act of cultural communication through her body. For example, Lesa Lockford's book *Performing Femininity* (2004) contains an entire chapter about her experience of stripping at a New Orleans nightclub. Lockford, who had been collecting the personal narratives of strippers and sex workers, was challenged to strip by an interviewee so that she might obtain bodily knowledge of this culture.

Most performative writers are autoethnographers. However, when a performative writer embodies voices other than her own, she is not creating an autoethnography. If one writes a personal narrative from another's perspective, then, is this a personal narrative, monologue, or story? As a performative writer, I have maintained two specific values in my work. First, I believe that all creative performative writing, whether or not it originates from another individual, must be carefully molded. Through an economy of words, the writer should convey a message that penetrates an audience's psyche, and leaves them in a state of self-examination. Through symbolism or metaphor or dramatic devices, a story should promote self-reflection.

My second value is implied in the first. Creative, performative writing should be written for an audience. The narratives, stories, or monologues should express a philosophical or spiritual belief system that the writer wishes to convey in her work. For me, that belief system has been developed through my understanding and experience with the primary narrative. In the next section, I will explore the definition of the primary narrative and how I have used the primary narrative in my performative work.

## THE PRIMARY NARRATIVE

Storytelling is one of the most fascinating human activities. Through stories, we transmit values, build interpersonal relationships, grow, heal, and possibly alter our future. Stories have the power to change how we think or feel, how we respond to others. Many of us can recall at least one story that may have changed our behavior or current actions. But the stories we tell can often serve as pieces of literature. Each of us edits the stories we tell to others—changing, embellishing, or omitting details. In a sense, we are all conversational fiction writers. If we were to tell the actual details of an event, such as the experience of seeing a film with a friend, we would be likely to exclude such details as the time and location of the film, what, if anything, we ate while watching the film, the weather, the ticket line. We would be more likely to share what we thought of the film or how the film may have reminded us of real life or another film. We edit our stories to make ourselves interesting and engaging to others.

Amidst all these stories, which compose the fiction of our lives, we have specific life stories that we tell over and over to ourselves and to others because we spend our lifetimes coping with the facts that comprise our identities. In a qualitative research study (Carilli, 1990), I interviewed individuals about the experience of coming to terms with some type of abuse. One of the conclusions from this study is that individuals will repeat stories of abuse as part of coming to terms with that abuse. While doing the study, I began to realize that most stories which we repeat demonstrate some degree of abuse, either physical or emotional violence.

When I began teaching public speaking at an Illinois university, I was given remedial classes, which consisted mostly of students from Chicago's south or west sides, predominately African American areas reputed for poverty and gang violence. I remember the frustration I experienced by attempting to teach these students the models of public speaking—which do not acknowledge orality or the value of stories in speech making. One day, I abandoned the lesson and just asked the students to tell a story of something which moved or affected them. One student told a story of his best friend's death. The friend had been mistakenly identified and shot. In extraordinary detail, the student shared his experience watching his friend die in his arms. As the students released their stories, the classroom climate changed, and I realized that I would not be able to reach them with the textbook. They were eloquent speakers—performative speakers who used rules and models that did not fit in traditional public speaking texts.

I took this knowledge into all of my classes—no matter what I taught—because I started to understand that some individuals never will be open to learning if they do not have the opportunity to tell their stories. Thus, one of my goals has been to create that opportunity for students to tell their stories, if not in the classroom, then to me. I encourage the telling because the telling assists in purging. I understood the importance of purging what I call my "primary narrative." I began that purging process in therapy and continued it in graduate school. In a course called "Writing as Performance" where we were encouraged to write performance texts by embodying the texts out loud, I wrote a text called "Big Boy." Here is an excerpt from that text:

### JOE

You really wanna know about my fightin' days. I'll tell you then. I was born in Hartford, this big street kid, back during the Depression. My parents were a couple of Sicilian immigrants—arranged marriage here in America. I took up boxing to help make a couple of bucks for the family. I had eight brothers and sisters. I was good at boxing and my friends gave me a nickname, "Big Boy," 'cause I was big and had a boyish face. I hated that god-damned name, always did. My real name is Umberto. My mother named me after the king of Italy at the time. My brother changed my name *to "Joe"* because back then, in the 1940s, who ever heard of a boxer named Umberto. That was a sissy name. *Joe* Big Boy.

### DAUGHTER

See this crack on the wall? This was one of the Christmas cracks. This one here was an Easter crack. When I was a kid, Mom used to hang my artwork over the cracks that Dad used to make—either with his fist or his head. After awhile there were so many cracks, Mom stopped putting up my artwork. It looked more natural that way. He'd get mad and he'd ram his head into the wall. Sometimes, but seldom, his fist. And if he was really mad, he'd get down on his hands and knees and smash his head into the metal radiators until it would bleed.

Twenty years ago when I wrote "Big Boy," I was exploring the way in which autobiography informs creative writing. For me, "Big Boy" was a study of how to script identity because it contains my primary narrative—the story of how I was traumatized by my father's violence during my childhood. "Big Boy" explores the immigrant struggle while also providing a critique of boxing.

In the process of attempting to script identity, a primary narrative guides each of us through our life experiences. This primary narrative is the source of our identity, the defining event (and sometimes events) of our lives. Often, this component of identity has a cultural foundation—whether that foundation is an identity with a group or with a belief system. Sometimes that story might have many incarnations, but it is the same story we tell over and over to others and ourselves, often seeking resolution or some way to make sense of our lives. For me, that story was about growing up with a father who was an ex-boxer. My experiences with my father affected every part of my life. One way I have been able to address this primary narrative is through performative writing, where I tell a version of this narrative. But another way I have addressed my foundational experience is by embodying other individuals in my performative work. I write from others' perspectives because it helps me to understand and to come to terms with my primary narrative. In "Big Boy" the daughter explains, "Once you see someone break a wall down just once, you realize you have a lot to be happy about." Rendering stories that allow for feelings of connection and engagement with others can promote resolve. This has led me to write monologues and narratives from others' perspectives. One of my most recent collections of monologues is called *Permanent Damage*, a self-reflexive examination of my primary narrative.

Writing this collection has brought me to a location where I understand the value and importance of the primary narrative. When I write from others' perspectives, I locate a way to repeat and access my own primary narrative. Each text is a metaphorical punch, blow, jab—something that brings me back to my source, back to my primary narrative.

> My father was an ex-boxer. My father knocked out Joe Louis. He achieved this at my expense. I grew up with a father who either plowed into or tore down the walls of my psyche. My father sabotaged my spirit and my life has been reclamation of that spirit.

In each of the six monologues in *Permanent Damage,* the narrators find themselves in their present circumstances by going to their primary narratives—understanding the present by reclaiming the past. In the following two examples from *Permanent Damage*, "Some Other Dimension" and "The Circus Lady," each narrator attempts to come to terms with her relationship with her deceased mother. Each narrator puts herself into a reverberating situation, reminiscent of her relationship with her mother:

## SOME OTHER DIMENSION

(to the audience) How can you tell if a pair of sneakers fits you? (This can also be improvised.) How long does it take to break them in? OK. I had my last good pair of sneakers when I was in my late 20's—about the same time I became an actress, or shall I say, that's when I began to take acting seriously. Before that I hung around doing odd jobs—computer work and such. It was about the same time I met Jay. She was working at the computer company and we just felt an immediate bond. She had done some acting. I don't think I could ever have become an actress without Jay—well and Louise, too. Louise was her lover. Jay was the first person who helped me take myself seriously. (pause) I'm straight but I have to admit, I found myself looking at Jay, becoming, well, curious, and Louise—well, Louise reminded me a lot of my father. My father was a college professor before he retired and he had this way about him. He was Greek—well—Greek descent, and he'd come up to you and pinch your cheek. And his sisters—they were all the same. "ooggyy, ooggyy, ooggyy," they'd say. No matter how old you were, they'd treat you like you were a newborn. But I liked that because they were expressive. My mother was a lot like Jay, annoyed by all this expressiveness, and my father would tease her unmercifully because he just knew how much she hated to be teased. She was a WASP and proud of that fact. I don't know why she married my father, but they did have a great life together.

I met Jay shortly after my mother's death. I was living with Henry at the time. (amused) Good old reliable Henry. He was just gorgeous but he was almost, how can I say this, um, too liberal. He believed in openness about everything, so he knew I had a crush on Jay, and he'd let me stay over and sleep at their apartment. (pause) Nothing really happened. (assertively) I do prefer men, but, if I were going to do anything with a woman, it would have been Jay. It got close and it got scary. I loved them both, and I didn't want anything to happen to either of them. I think I was probably in a really hard space at the time.

(very sadly, but trying not to show her feelings of devastation) I still remember very vividly the day my mother died. She had cancer and I knew she was dying, but I just couldn't accept it. I was 20 years old, and she seemed so strong, so infallible, so sturdy, like nothing could shake her. I was away at school, and my dad called and said, "you'd better get home." I knew what it meant. I just couldn't bring myself to see her, to actually see her, so instead, when I got home, I took a bike ride. I put on that pair of sneakers I was telling you about, they were new at the time, and I rode about 50 miles and I just didn't look back. I didn't stop. I didn't breathe. I just kept on going. My body hurt so bad I could barely see, but I kept on riding my bike like if I rode far enough, it just wouldn't happen, she just wouldn't die, or I'd ride into some other dimension and she'd be there, waiting for me. (swallows hard, a long pause) When I got home that night, they told me she had passed away, and I was so tired, I just fell asleep and woke up the next day. My dad's heart was just broken. I never knew he could cry like that. He touched me on the shoulder and told me I was just lucky to have had someone who loved me so deeply. (upset, somewhat angry, slowly) I just wish I could go there. I wish I could go to that place—where she went and speak to her through some kind of, I don't know, translator or something. I just know it exists. I know it does.

(regains herself) When Louise and Jay broke up, I admit, it was tough for me. Louise was like my father and Jay was like my mother. Louise took the breakup hard. She never thought Jay would leave her and she talked about it—just like my father. (confidently) You know, some people, they keep their feelings to themselves, and I think that's a good thing because people who wear their heart on their sleeve, well, (pause) they just have a harder time. They just do. I went to the docks with Louise. Just me and her and she was carrying on about Jay, and it just tore me up, and I started to sob. I just sobbed and sobbed. She looked at me helplessly. After that, I didn't see Louise anymore. (pause) But I saw Jay a lot. Our friendship just continued to grow. It was Jay that encouraged me to go into the theater. She thought I just had a really dramatic side. And the funny thing is I get that side from my father (emphasizes) not my mother, but my father. The first time I appeared in a show, he came up to me afterwards, and pinched my cheek and said, "ooggyy, ooggyy, ooggyy." What else could he say? I knew he was proud of me because in many ways, I really take after him.

## THE CIRCUS LADY

My stories are always conversation stoppers. Here's what I mean. (pause) My first husband is now a woman. The day he called to tell me I was just shocked. Imagine this large, strapping, hunk of a guy turning into a woman. What a pity! I suppose I was promoted or demoted with my second husband. He was only a transvestite. Another big guy—someone who in your wildest dreams, you could never imagine in woman's clothes. After our divorce, he married a former lesbian or as they say, "wasbian," which worked perfectly—she could be with a woman, and he could feel comfortable dressed up.

Since then, I can assure you, the men I date are very, very straight. For a while, I dated this cop named Carl, and he was very macho. One day, he thought, he'd play a joke on me and he put my bathrobe on—since he knew my history and all—and I just screamed. It took hours to console me. (pause) We broke up after a brief few months and that was fine. I was tired of sleeping at his apartment. He had all these shrunken head figures everywhere and that wasn't a good sign, I thought. So after him, I dated a guy who was almost 20 years younger than me. He was really cute and an aspiring musician, but I gave up on him because I just got tired of putting away his comic books. And everything to him was "cool, yeah, cool." And I just couldn't stand that—I simply couldn't. (pause, reflectively) And then I met Michael and really fell in love.

Now, here's where people tend to judge me. I saw Michael frequently on the street with a sign that said "homeless." He was begging for money, so one day I got the guts to ask him out for breakfast. I know he was panhandling, but he was just gorgeous—thick, dark, curly hair, a body that looked like it had been sculpted, and alright, his teeth were in bad shape, but he was damned sexy. So, I invited him over. And we started becoming friends, then we had sex, and I could feel myself falling in love with him. He had these precious blue eyes and he was just so sensitive. After a few weeks, he introduced me to his mother. She was a really friendly elderly woman who lived in a luxurious apartment on Lake Shore Drive. Most of the time, when he wasn't panhandling or with me, he'd be at her place. One time, I was alone with her and she warned me about him. She told me "he's not the great guy he seems to be." (pause) My own mother would never have said something like that to me. (sadly) God, my own mother never gave a shit about any of my boyfriends. When I was about six years old, she had a nervous breakdown and she was committed. After coming out of the mental hospital, she met some guy who made a living as a magician, and she took off with him to San Francisco, calling my siblings and me on occasion when she remembered our birthdays. So, I never saw very much of her. When she died, I felt like I was going to a stranger's funeral. Thank God for my father. (sighing) He was both a mother and father to me. (compassionately) I guess my mother just had a wild streak in her, which I attribute to the fact that her relatives were all in the circus. (pause) The only thing I ever had of hers was this ring she gave me on my 9th birthday. I keep it hidden away in my dresser drawer and I take it out when I feel nostalgic—when I miss her—when I wonder what she could have been like.

I never suspected that there was anything wrong with Michael other than having a bad bout of luck—which happens to all of us. But I began to suspect something when I took him to a dinner party and he fell asleep. I thought that was really an odd thing to do, but then I thought he just wasn't feeling well. After that, my friends didn't invite us back. They thought something was strange, like he was a dealer or something. And silly me, I told them they were being paranoid. (reluctantly) Then one day, while he was sleeping, I went to wash his shirt with my clothes and while I was cleaning out the pockets, I found a needle. When he woke up, he explained that he had a problem with heroin and that he was working really hard to get off the stuff. I was furious because he had put me at risk for AIDS, but he assured me he would never be that careless. So, I forgave him. I mean, he was trying. He explained it all to me—he was on a government program to get clean, and eventually he'd go back to work. Then one day when he wasn't there, I went to look at my mother's ring. I don't know why. I just had this feeling. (angry) It was missing. I became hysterical, and I called his mother, screaming and crying. She told me to calm down and come over. I went to her place, and she took me to a pawnshop where I would most likely find the ring. (annoyed) Sure enough, there it was. I had to pay $60 to get it out of hock. That's when I realized seeing Michael was not a good thing for me. So, I broke it off with him. He was pretty mad. (with disbelief) A few weeks later, I received a letter from him telling me I was lousy in bed. (determined) My feelings are this—I'd rather be a lousy fuck than a fuckin' lousy person. (pause) I never saw him again. I took my mother's ring and I hid it somewhere else. (painfully) It's all I have of her. And I can't let anything happen to it.

*Parents are our first intimate relationship. We learn about intimacy and nurturance from our parents. As I witnessed my father's rage, I became an observer. I left my body as a survival strategy, and I replaced it with other's lives. I live through others. By listening to their stories and embodying these stories, I am able to live in my life.*

With *Permanent Damage*, I am setting parameters for performative writers that can be distinguished from those of autoethnographic performative writers. My focus is on the structure of monologues and how monologues come to fruition through the writer's philosophy. With this in mind, I turn to the next section of this manuscript, which describes how I have used my knowledge as a performative writer to work with my students. After an explanation of how to script identity, I offer examples of former students who have scripted and performed their identities.

*Chapter Two*

# Scripting Identity Using the Primary Narrative

Scripting Identity is the process of bringing one's life into narrative form for the sake of public or private performance. When one scripts her identity, she is shaping her primary narrative into a creative text, which helps to explore an aspect of human communication, a segment of identity. For the sake of explanation and illustration, I will share how I have worked on this process of scripting identity with several students. With each individual, both the process and the result have been unique and specific to the individual.

The general process of scripting identity has four stages:

1. Accessing the Primary Narrative
2. Selecting the Genre to Complement the Primary Narrative
3. Performing the Script
4. Assessing How the Script has Affected the Individual/Scriptwriter

## ACCESSING THE PRIMARY NARRATIVE

Of all these stages, accessing the primary narrative is undoubtedly the most difficult. To assist writers in accessing their primary narrative requires self-disclosure and intimacy. When, however, we examine issues of performance and human behavior, we rely upon our experiences to guide our understanding. While working with students, I have become intimately acquainted with their life experiences. I value an understanding of how each individual moves through the world.

One method I have used to locate students' primary narratives is to have them write an extensive narrative that delves into the most significant events of their lives. I do not grade students on this assignment, and they have a choice as to whether or not I will actually read the narrative. Through this assignment, they reflect on those moments that molded their identities. I encourage them to examine these reflections and develop a research project based on an experience that deeply affected them. My first success with this assignment evolved into a student interviewing women who, like her, had lost their mothers at an early age. Interviewing these women brought some degree of resolve and peace-making with her loss.

Those who choose to script their identities usually recognize that connection which exists between art and life and wish to explore the artistic component of their lives. All the scripts in this compilation were developed from the discovery of each writer's primary narrative. Each scripting process was unique depending upon the writer and the primary narrative.

## SELECTING THE GENRE TO COMPLEMENT
## THE PRIMARY NARRATIVE

To script narrative requires a sensitivity and understanding of genre and the key role genre plays in the script. The scriptwriter must select the writing genre that best complements the message of the text. So, the scriptwriter must engage in the process of trying on genre. "Trying on" genre is similar to the experience of performers who play with character, "trying on" different vocal inflections, intonations, and movements. "Trying on" is the notion that one must fit comfortably into a piece of clothing, and furthermore, that piece of clothing must accurately reflect the individual. Creative writers and scriptwriters "try on" many different genres until they can find the one that fits best. Sometimes, the genre might seem like a perfect fit but must be returned or altered. Sometimes, the genre might intersect with another genre, like a change of costume during a performance.

I use the word "costume" to acknowledge the craft involved in being a scriptwriter. A costume is a specially designed article of clothing used for a performance. Like the performer who must be aware of the look, style, and color of his or her costume and what that costume conveys about character, the scriptwriter must be aware of what the genre conveys about the identity being scripted. Like costume, genre masks identity. Like costume, genre is façade. Yet, genre is the structure that allows the authentic autobiographical text to emerge. Costume allows character to reveal him or herself.

The new identity, which presents itself in costume, has been molded and shaped into a script. If not for the costume, if not for the genre, all utterances might be considered scripts and performances. Here are three questions I raise to assist scriptwriters in their selection of costume or genre:

1. What genre complements the cultural experience of the identity being scripted?
According to Victor Turner (1986), each individual may belong to several star groups or cultures. At particular times, individuals might find themselves more aligned with one of those star groups. For example, at times, I am more aligned with Italian American culture, and at other times, with lesbian culture. Homophobic Italian Americans create tremendous cognitive dissonance for me because I am thrown into a collision of cultures.

In the process of scripting identity, the scriptwriter will locate that culture or star group that is at the core of the primary narrative. This culture, with its own set of rules and values, must be rendered as part of the script. The scriptwriters must sensitively select the genre that allows entry into their cultural experiences and into their primary narratives. I will discuss the process of genre selection with each specific script.

2. What genre will validate the experiences of the scriptwriter?
The scriptwriters must locate a genre that validates their experiences. In short, they must create a cultural world where they and their range of experiences fit or make sense. There must be a particular logic or pattern to the genre that will allow for some degree of coming to terms with the primary narrative. The process of scripting identity should invite an inner dialogue for the scriptwriters, which allows them to heal or to make peace with a part of themselves.

3.To what extent will the scriptwriter reflectively engage so that s/he might reach the appropriate genre?
The scriptwriters must fully and reflectively engage every part of themselves to locate the genre most appropriate for their scripts. At the point the scriptwriter selects the genre; s/he should feel the choice to be intuitive or natural. To reach a point where the genre choice feels intuitive or natural, the scriptwriter has incubated with the primary narrative so that the framework emerges as an overall component of identity.

## PERFORMING THE SCRIPT

The scriptwriter decides if s/he wishes to take the script to the next level—public performance, or if s/he feels comfortable in some degree of self-resolution. Public performance has the potential to validate others who share components of the scriptwriter's identity and can be a strong and meaningful experience for audience members. I advise, however, that the script should be one that reaches a marginalized culture rather than a mainstream culture whose voice is validated regularly in the mainstream media. Audience members who do not share components of the scriptwriter's identity have the opportunity to learn about a culture or voice that has been silenced.

By performing this script, the scriptwriter becomes a humanitarian or an activist, promoting understanding and tolerance of a culture. By changing someone's views about a culture, the scriptwriter encourages action, or that the audience members change their behavior toward members of the culture being advocated in the performance.

## ASSESSING HOW THE SCRIPT HAS AFFECTED THE INDIVIDUAL/SCRIPTWRITER

With each of the scripts that I present, the scriptwriter changes over time. Usually, the script politicizes the performer. By embodying the script, the scriptwriter/performer re-emerges with new insight about him or her and with a desire to share such bodily knowledge with others.

## THE SCRIPTS

The following scripts reflect key components of the authors' identities. With the exception of one of the authors, all of the authors of these scripts were born and raised in northwest Indiana, known for its steel industry. For the most part, the scripts reflect a working-class ethnic sensibility and contain a primary narrative. In each of the primary narratives, the authors are attempting to work through or come to some understanding about their lives. For each of these authors, the process of scripting identity was arduous and emotionally challenging.

In "Deconstructing the Oreo," Adrienne Viramontes showcases several performative narratives that, when woven together, illuminate her experience of growing up as a Latina in a motherless environment. For Viramontes, her primary narrative, the loss of her mother as a young child, has meant a disconnection with her Mexican American culture. Viramontes' grandparents, who raised her, immigrated to northwest Indiana to work in the steel mills. Her rich personal history of immigration serves as the backdrop for the loss of her mother.

Dave Fanno's "The Coke Plant" is a lively, descriptive accounting of his early years working in the steel mills. A descendant of Italian immigrants,

Fanno overcomes his plight of serving in "the coke plant" at the steel mill by returning to school. For Fanno, the expectation for him to work in the steel mill serves as a primary narrative that changes and alters his perceptions of having a far different future.

"A Letter To Sam," written by Jennifer Bianchi, is based on a collection of interview narratives about single-motherhood. In addition to writing her own personal narrative, Bianchi interviewed single-mother family members and edited the interviews for performance. For Bianchi, this collection of familial narratives underscores her choice to be a single-mother. Bianchi works through her primary narrative of understanding and embracing this choice.

Erin Okamoto Protsman's "Without Due Process" reflects how historical events can affect identity. By exploring the experiences of her family members who were interned in camps during the Japanese internment of World War II, Okamoto Protsman attempts to explain how ethnicity shapes identity. This video gives an extraordinary accounting of family members' daily lives in the camps, how they survived this ordeal, and how they feel about being interned as Japanese Americans. By giving voice to her family members in this video, Okamoto Protsman deciphers her own experience of being from a marginalized ethnic group.

Ami Kleminski's autoethnography, "I Am Not Contained between My Boots and My Hat," is a vivid examination of gender roles in the steel mills. For Kleminski, working in the mills and reflecting on her life there yields an understanding of how she experiences gender. Kleminski, by her own admission, states her primary narrative to be that of seeking female approval. Because of her desire for female approval, she provides a unique and descriptive look at everyday life in a traditionally male-dominated trade. Through this lens, Kleminski gives an honest rendering of being a woman or in a steel environment.

Bill Boggs' narratives "June Bug's House" and "Photographs and Memories" demonstrate how the author understands his relationship to others based on his relationship with his father. In "June Bug's House," Boggs explains how his upbringing taught him that manhood was equated with rage, violence, and alcoholism. Boggs explores his process of unlearning this particular definition of manhood. His foray into this new understanding takes him back to his original primary narrative in "Photographs and Memories" where he attempts to resolve his early understanding of manhood.

# Chapter Three

# Adrienne Viramontes: I Had Been A White Reflection

## Script One: Deconstructing the Oreo

*I first met Adrienne Viramontes in the office of my colleague. Viramontes was a public relations major, and my colleague was the advisor for all public relations students. He introduced Viramontes as an extraordinary storyteller. Viramontes took an oral interpretation class with me. Her work was very impressive, as she made clear, polished performance choices to complement her interpretations of literary texts. Performance seemed effortless for her.*

*At the time I met Viramontes, I was co-editing a book on media depictions of ethnic groups while teaching several courses in ethnic studies. Having been politicized by understanding how my own ethnicity affected my life, I encouraged students to examine the role that ethnicity played in their lives. Though I knew Viramontes was Mexican American, she rarely talked about her ethnicity. She would shrug off any discussion of her background or personal history.*

*Later, as a graduate student in a qualitative methods class, Viramontes interviewed her grandmother for an assignment on conversation. One day on my way into my office, I heard the tape-recorded interview with the elderly woman. Her grandmother was telling some fascinating stories about her own personal history—stories about her grandmother's escape from Mexico, how Mexicans were treated in America, how the Spaniards treated the Mexicans ("never taint the blood, never taint the blood"). Viramontes and I talked about this interview and the valuable information it contained as a piece of oral history, a narrative, and a story of life imitating art. But still, she resisted any talk about this interview as part of her own identity. She examined it as a peripheral text with cultural meaning for others, not her.*

*Finally, Viramontes traveled to meet some friends in Kentucky. While at a restaurant, one of her friends called to her attention her "brownness," a characteristic that was not commonly witnessed in restaurants in that particular*

21

*region. From that moment on, Viramontes began to explore the implications of "brownness."*

*I encouraged her to write stories about her experiences growing up. She took the assignment seriously and began to write stories that were oral in nature—performative, entertaining, and poignant. Oral, performative narratives were an appropriate genre for this project because they captured her culture's orality.*

*What happened during Viramontes' process allowed her to delve deeper into her own ethnicity. In addition to sharing her experience of understanding her juvenile diabetes, Viramontes shared her childhood pain of losing her mother. When this component of her identity was released, a loss which I see as her primary narrative, her ability to explore and understand her ethnicity followed. She began to understand how she lost touch with her ethnicity upon losing her mother. This became a critical juncture for her—loss of her mother meant disconnection with her ethnicity.*

*Viramontes created four lengthy narratives about her experiences of growing up Latina in a text called "Deconstructing The Oreo," which she performed. For her to continue on a path of personal growth and realization, developing this text was essential.*

*Viramontes has performed the text several times with continuous modifications being made to the ending, depending upon her current situation. She uses minimal props and suggests change in character through space. Each character—mother, grandmother, great-grandmother, and herself, has a specific location on stage. This allows the audience to distinguish each story.*

## DECONSTRUCTING THE OREO

*There is a large screen so that the audience can see a video with a picture of an elderly couple. The following poem is pre-recorded and played when the picture appears.*

I rescued my grandmother tonight.

Not from death, or malnutrition, not from fire or from any accident.

I rescued her from her husband.

He's not traditionally abusive, at least, not any more.

He doesn't drink or smoke, although it would probably help.

He's just 94 and conveniently crazy during prime time television.

Her blood boils each night around 7:00.

While America is laughing at re-runs of Seinfeld, my grandmother is dying inside.

She tries to drown her sorrows in cheesy Mexican programs.

While my grandfather asks her for the 26th time if the water bill was paid, or when the social security checks will come in the mail.

He knows damn well when they arrive, since they have arrived at the same time for the past 30 years. But he continues to drive her to a personal hell.

It's bad when old people go crazy. It's worse when only one partner is crazy and the other is left to baby sit.

While she sits on the couch, she thinks about the past.

What a waste her life has been no matter how we try to disagree with her.

She thinks about how he has never showered more than once a week, even when he worked in the steel mills.

How she used to have to sleep next to his smelly body for sixty years.

How he would force that smelly body of his on top of hers at his convenience.

And, when she would try to refuse his advances, he would kick her out of the bed, onto the floor.

How she would wake him up in the middle of the night crying because she knew she was pregnant.

How she waited for her turn next to a woman who bled to death after she received an abortion in a run-down apartment.

She thinks about every meal she has ever cooked for him.

Each time she has had to look at his food while he was chewing it with his mouth open.

When he belches in the middle of each meal to inform her he is full.

Those were some of the good days.

She remembers the bad days too.

When he would get so angry he would beat their son with a belt until he bled.

He never bought her a gift for any occasion. He just gave her money, like a whore.

She thinks about how she left her first husband, who beat her and abused her verbally.

Whom she had to escape from with her first child so that he wouldn't catch her.

And for what?

So she could marry him. A man she thought was different, kind, and generous.

She remembers the letter she received from his "sister" who ended up being his wife that he abandoned in Mexico many years ago.

She thinks about how stupid she is. How blind she was. How miserable she is for keeping his secret for so many years.

Each night from 7–10:00. She sits on the couch and re-lives her life.

Tonight I rescued her for a few hours. I sat between them.

When I'm there he doesn't act up.

He doesn't clap his hands loudly so she can't hear the television.

When I'm there he knows better than to walk up to her and threaten to punch her in the face. At 94 machismo is alive and well.

He can't kick her out of HIS house, HIS bed or demand the keys to HIS car.

He knows that when I'm there, I will call the ambulance when my grandmother is close to death.

At least tonight she could just sit there and watch TV.

At least tonight, I could do more than just take her to the grocery store.

Tonight, I rescued her from the perils of prime time television.

I wish she had the strength to rescue herself from everything else.

*As the poem ends, lights come up on performer who is sitting down stage right. She begins her narrative.*

My grandma was not always so sad. I can remember her telling me stories of moments in time when she was happy. At 80, she only has memories.

She knows what it's like to be an immigrant, to be Latina, to be a survivor.

My grandma is a survivor.

I think that surviving is what being Mexican is all about.

Then again, I'm not really sure.

What I am sure of is that my grandmother learned how to survive from her grandmother, Gabriella. I guess it runs in the family.

*Performer walks from stage right to stage left where she is surrounded by a hanging noose.*

Her name was Gabriella Lozano. She would have been my great-great grandmother. Ever since I was a kid, my grandma would tell me that she loved Gabriella more than her own mother. I never understood why she felt that way. Gabriella owned a lot of land in Mexico during the early 1900's. She was the only woman in Mexico who owned anything or was worth anything in the city of Michuacan, where she lived. She had married a man who loved booze and gambling as much as he loved her. And sometimes that was a problem. He would often disappear for days, gambling all of their money away, and sometimes, all of his clothing. When her husband had been missing for a few days, Gabriella got her horse ready, tied her skirt in a knot, and rode into town to find him. And find him she did. He was sitting in a bar, naked and broke. She entered the saloon and dragged her naked husband home on the back of her horse. That was the day the men in town thought she had gone too far.

The next day, while she was tending to the horses and cows, some of the local men grabbed her, tied a rope around her neck, and hung her. They demanded all of her money. Gabriella tried to tell them that she had none, but these men didn't know that land was worth more than money. They would let her rest while she caught her breath and then hang her again, each time thinking that she would give in. When the men finally let her down, they promised that they would return the next day to finish the job and that Gabriella should have her money ready for them, or she would die hanging from her own tree, on her own land.

The next day, Gabriella was on her way to America by way of the Rio Grande. You could still see the marks around her neck from where the rope had burned through her skin. For the rest of her life she would wear high-neck dresses in order to hide her scars.

That day Gabriella, her daughter Maria, and my grandma, who was only a baby, escaped from Mexico with only the clothing on their backs. In America, things would be better. When I heard that story I took pride in the knowledge that my great-great grandmother had a monstrous set of balls. She reminded me of my own mother because they both believed in marrying within Mexican culture. "Never taint the blood. Never taint the blood." My grandmother followed orders and married a Mexican. And spent the rest of her life telling me about how much she regretted it. But my mom never mentioned that.

Instead, my mom used to dance around the house while she listened to Mariachi music. Watching my mom dance reminded me of a woman dancing her way through a bullfight.

*Performer dances in a circle at front of stage*

Her favorite song was this one called "Volver, Volver." I don't say the words very well because I don't speak Spanish, but I know that they mean— "come back, come back." And I was always wondering what they wanted me to come back to, but I would worry about that later. Besides, if I wanted to know anything that bad my mom would tell me. She was nice like that.

My mom taught me the basics of childhood—these rules were important, yet very simple. 1. Don't sing in the car. That's what radios are for. 2. Don't wipe your eyes after touching a jalapeno pepper—that one should be pretty self-explanatory. 3. Don't have a birthday without a piñata. And, 4. Always be home on time to watch *General Hospital*. Apparently, this was the most important of all.

*Performer sits down in chair center stage*

When I was 5, I used to come home from kindergarten and look forward to sitting in the living room with my mom while she drank her coffee. She used to let me drink coffee too. Unlike her, I didn't take my coffee black. I preferred mine with cream and lots of sugar. I felt important holding a cup of coffee in my hands. I used to pretend that people were looking at me drinking coffee. I know I looked good holding the cup to my lips, making those sippy sounds, and crossing my legs as if my feet touched the floor. I was five years old, drinking coffee in the middle of the afternoon and watching *General Hospital* with my mom. Now this is what real women did.

Coffee was a huge part of my home life, and in the first grade, had become a part of my education. My first grade teacher had instructed us to decorate an empty coffee can so that we could put our pens and pencils inside of it. Grownups have an odd fixation with storage—well anyway, my teacher, Ms. Baranko, was telling us a story in class, and this boy that sat across from me was poking holes in the lid of his coffee can. It seemed like a good idea, so I did the same. It was cathartic to puncture the plastic. What was once a perfect container with an airtight lid was now damaged goods, unusable and very beautiful. Unfortunately, Ms. Baranko did not agree. She was an intimidating woman, but her intimidation was nothing in comparison to her disappointment in me.

She was going to make sure that I learned my lesson, so she made me stay after school and sit in an empty room with her. I spent about 30 minutes listening to her breathe through her tight nasal passages, and I could hear her panty hose rub together as she walked around the room ignoring me.

Conversation must really be a reward, because when you disobey, people stop talking to you.

Apparently she never bothered to call my mom and tell her that I would be late. So, when I didn't show up at home to drink my coffee and watch *General Hospital*, my mom came looking for me at school. And the first place she looked was Ms. Baranko's room.

*Performer gets up from chair and walks up stage slightly left*

When I saw my mom enter the classroom I thought I was in big trouble. She started asking Ms. Baranko why I was here and why she never called her. Ms. Baranko tried to tell me my mom what a felon I was for destroying a plastic lid. But, my mom reminded Ms. Baranko that it was only a coffee can. And, since we had plenty of coffee at home, her daughter could poke holes in any goddamn coffee can she wanted.

Suddenly Ms. Baranko did not seem as smart, or as intimidating. And that was the day I learned that if you had a better argument than someone else did, you could poke holes in anything.

*Performer walks to the center*

Words were very easy to conquer, but silence was a different kind of war. And nothing breeds more silence than disease. I became a diabetic when I was five, and my mom used to tell me that only "special" people got insulin shots. Every morning I would run into the bathroom so that I could get my "special" shot. I never realized that my life depended on it. So when my mom was diagnosed with an acute form of leukemia, I thought nothing of it. She went through something called chemotherapy. She was going to get some special shots too. I would accompany her to the hospital where they would inject her in her hip. She would smile at me while she bent over. On the way home from her treatment, she would vomit in a silver pan while she drove at the same time. As far as I could tell, there was nothing cute about leukemia, and the word "special" began to make me feel like I was running out of time. It never seemed to bother her.

She was in remission for a year and then she died. The last time I saw her she was gliding past the Christmas tree on a gurney with a plastic cup over her mouth. The men who drove the ambulance were pushing her out the door. The leukemia was eating my mother up and she could no longer live at home. I knew that Christmas morning would be the last time I would see her. She had no last words for me and I had none for her—something I would grow to regret for the rest of my life.

The day after she died, I wanted to be by myself so I could cry. But, the grownups that I lived with would not leave me alone. I could not cry in front of them because I noticed that it was harder for them to console me than it was for me to mourn. My tears seemed to remind them that I was a motherless child and that somehow my life would never be the same. So I stopped crying. I learned how to keep my face still and force the water back into my eyes. If my mother's death didn't bother me, then it wouldn't bother anyone.

When people die, it gets weird. No one talks to you unless they absolutely have to, and everybody is constantly on the phone. The air seems thick, and the house you live in seems like a prison. Time gets slower. Everywhere you go you remember the last time you saw the dead person—how she was standing in the kitchen talking on the baby blue rotary phone, lying in her bed, or sitting in her favorite black chair. All I could remember was that baby blue phone ringing, my grandma answering it and then crying. She walked over to me, sat down next to me, and told me that my mom was gone. I sat there in the dark, looking out the window, and got ready for the changes to come.

And they came pretty quickly. It was almost over—we just had to get through the wake and the funeral, and then I could stop worrying about everybody.

The only thing my grandmother seemed to be concerned with was what I would wear to the wake. She picked out a fashionable black and white velvet outfit, with a matching beret. She kept telling me how my mom would have wanted me to look nice for everyone. This line of reasoning would be used for the rest of my life—each time I would do something that they did not agree with—which was most of the time. So I put the uncomfortable outfit on and went to the funeral home for my final performance.

It was like a party. There were flowers and ribbons everywhere. There were a lot of people, and everyone was laughing and having a good time. I was, too. I ran up and down the stairs with my cousin and kept thinking how easy the whole funeral part was. If I stayed away from the coffin, it wasn't that bad. We were told to sit down because it was time for the priest to say some words, and then something very strange happened.

*A picture of the performer as a little girl looking at her mother appears. After one minute it will fade.*

I watched everyone in my family go up to the coffin and kiss her. When my grandma approached the casket, her knees buckled, and someone had to help her back to her chair. That woman is dramatic till the very end.

It was now my turn. My dad picked me up so that I could reach her cheek. And suddenly, I had a strange aerial view of her body and face. This was not my mother.

She was wearing so much makeup. For the first time, she wore lipstick, too much color on her cheeks, and a powdery film on her face. She looked like she had just gotten back from Acapulco. Her face was tan and her hands were gray. As my dad directed my face toward her cheek, I puckered my lips and made contact.

She was very cold. I didn't know you got cold when you died. Her eyes didn't move underneath the lids, and I remember thinking how big her pores were. I kissed her quickly and wanted to be put down. My lips tasted like makeup, and for the first time I couldn't cry. I couldn't believe my dad made me perform the kiss of death.

I don't remember anything else after that except that my dad was carrying my orange samsonite suitcases to my grandma's car and that I was moving in with my grandparents, because, again, my mom would have wanted it that way. I arrived at her house knowing that this time it was more than a visit with grandma—this was now my home. I walked into the house, sat on the couch and asked my grandma, "Am I yours now?"

*Home movies appear on the screen for three minutes. Lights come up on the performer as she continues to stand and speak to the audience*

Since visiting grandma and grandpa was always fun, I had high expectations of living with them. I thought that they would always be nice to me and give me presents when they walked through the door. However, I was beginning to learn the meaning of "nice place to visit—wouldn't want to live there."

I had not yet met any new friends, and the way my grandmother was dressing me for the winter was not helping. Each day I left the house, my grandma made sure that my head was covered. The hat that separated me from the normal people covered my entire head, and the connecting scarf was crisscrossed over my face and tied in the back of my head. Each day I arrived at the bus stop, I looked like I had a "cross your heart bra" on my face and a hat to match. But there was a reason for this.

I soon learned that there was a reason for everything—whether it made sense or not. If I caught a cold, it was always my fault. I either (a) didn't have my feet covered properly. Everybody knows that a cold starts in your feet and travels to your nose. (b) must have left the house with wet hair, because everybody knows that a wet head causes your pores to open and the cold germs find their way in. Or, (c) my shirt must not have been buttoned up high enough, because I obviously caught a draft in my chest, and everybody knows that a cold starts in your chest. Nothing in our house was contagious. Being healthy was only a matter of being practical, and I was never practical enough.

The reason I know this is because my grandma told me every day. She told me a lot of things . . . like you can't make a silk purse out of a sow's ear. This one meant that country people could never escape being country people. They always looked like they lived on a farm. They left doors open because they were born in a barn; they were the only people who should wear blue jeans and tennis shoes. Feet were not supposed to be bare, especially when dancing. My grandmother would say this one when my grandpa was around. He grew up on a farm, and she enjoyed reminding him of that.

"Waste not, want not." This meant that each time I threw away food the starving kids in Europe couldn't eat. If I didn't bother to pick up pennies that I dropped, I was wasting them and according to the adage, I would someday want for them. To this day, I make it a point to throw away pennies. It makes me feel good when I hear them hit the bottom of the garbage.

"Why buy the cow when you can get the milk free?" This meant that any woman who had sex, got pregnant, or was easy, was a slut—plain and simple—

a slut. This saying even included girls who hung out too long in the street in front of our house. Sluts—all of them—sluts. I was not allowed to hang out too much in the street. Although my friends were always outside, I was rarely allowed to spend too much time with them. My grandma hated them. They wore jeans, went barefoot, and were well on their way to becoming sluts.

I would be a good girl, someone who could cook and bake and knew how to clean and serve others. I would soon learn that there was only one way to do everything.

I learned the proper way to do the dishes, change the sheets, clean the house, do the laundry, clean my room, and clean the shower walls after each shower. There was even one way to get dressed. You start with your socks, then your pants, shirt and accessories. I kept asking her what difference it made which item went on first? As long as you left the house fully clothed what difference did it make? What if you changed your mind about something and your socks suddenly didn't match? But "changing your mind" was not an option for my grandmother.

She was going to train me just as her mother had trained her. I would learn everything it took to become a proper Mexican woman. She kept telling me that I should always tell her the truth no matter how bad it was. Nice girls were honest and slutty girls were liars. But I had a very hard time remembering all of the rules.

One morning as I got ready for school, I was preparing cereal for breakfast. I poured my cornflakes and went to grab the milk. My grandma was always watching me. She would approve of my room, check the shower walls to make sure I dried them, watch me wash the dishes so that I would not waste water, and of course she was watching me now pouring cereal. She was going to teach me the proper way to pour milk into a full bowl, so not to spill and especially, not to waste. I grabbed the milk from the refrigerator and tilted it so I could pour, and a little splash entered the bowl. She asked me if I had poured the milk yet and I thought she meant had I had finished filling the bowl. So I said no. She walked over to me and checked the bowl, saw the wet flakes and slammed my bowl down on the counter. She told me that she hated liars. She began to cry and told me that no matter how bad the truth was that I should always tell the truth. She didn't care what it was—just tell the truth. She explained to me that if she ever caught me in a lie again, I would not be in her heart anymore. She wouldn't know my name anymore, and she would cut me out of her memory. This is what her mom told her, and this is what would happen to girls in Mexico who didn't follow the rules.

That was the day I learned that the truth was stronger than love. And that nothing in life was simple, not even a bowl of cereal.

At night I wondered if my mom was watching me. She had to be up there in heaven, and so she had to hear me pray. I used to pray a lot after my mom died. I used to ask God to let her come and visit me as a ghost. I always thought I'd wake up one night and my mom's head would be in the corner of my room with a scarf around her neck, moving as if the wind were blowing. But God never answered my prayers and my mom never visited me. But maybe if I received my Holy Communion, it would all change. I would be good enough for God to finally talk to me and finally let my mom come and visit me.

You see, my grandmother promised my mom (on her deathbed) that I would receive my Holy Communion. I was sent to St. Edward's Church where they taught me to read the Bible and pray on a Rosary and after I completed the program, I would get to stand in line and eat a white cracker. I had seen people waiting in line for this cracker every Sunday at church. It was just like a wedding march, and the cracker probably tasted good like wedding cake. But in order to get the cracker, I had to talk to a man behind a wall and tell him all of the things I did wrong.

When I sat down in the confessional, I could see the priest through diamond shaped holes in the wall. I tried to see his eyes and his hair—it was hard. Why was he hiding? Was telling the truth supposed to be easier if you couldn't see his face? I told him that I had lied to my grandma that week. I didn't keep my room very clean, and I was disrespectful to my grandfather because every time he told me something, I would ask him, "why?" I was embarrassed because my sins didn't seem very worthy, and I could only think of three things that I should be forgiven for.

I thought about how stupid I must have sounded in the confessional. Big deal—I lied and was messy. I watched *Sixty Minutes* every week. Those people on that show had some real sins—robbery, murder, fraud—the works. I thought earning my cracker was going to be a much bigger deal than it was. So when I stood in line with my white dress and pearls and opened my mouth, I was devastated when I tasted what I had waited three years for.

It definitely was not a cracker, and it sure didn't taste like wedding cake. It tasted like plastic—I could feel the seam of the wafer on my tongue as I trapped it in my mouth. I walked away from the priest trying to chew the plastic wafer and pretend that it was all worth it. But it wasn't. When I got home from my Holy Communion, I cut up my dress and threw my Bible in my closet. I was never going back to church again. It was clear that when my mom died, God stopped acknowledging me, and I was never going to ask anything from him ever again.

A few weeks later, my grandma found my cut-up dress in the closet. She was really mad at me. What kind of girl cuts up her clothes? Didn't I have any respect for her? With habits like mine, what kind of man would want me? She reminded me that if her mother would have found my cut-up dress, I would have found my teeth on the floor, or since I cut the dress with my hands, she would have beaten them with a rolling pin. Apparently, my great-grand-mother was one of those "eye-for-an-eye" people.

Over the years I had heard many stories of my great grandmother. She died before my parents met, so luckily, I never had to meet her. I was told that she would have never liked me because I was a girl, and girls were useless. I was told that if she had raised me, she would have beaten my hands with a rolling pin if I didn't make a perfectly round tortilla, or fold the clothes properly. Her husband, my grandma's father, had left them many different times, for many different women, and they hated him.

Her name was Maria Moreno. She was with Gabriella the day she left Mex-ico. They were lucky enough to find a man who would carry them across the river to America. Maria cradled my grandmother in her arms as her feet touched the top of the Rio Grande. I believe that was the last kind act she showed my grandmother, who was only 13 months old and not yet old enough to abuse.

By the time my grandma was three, her mother Maria began to train her to be a "good Mexican girl." She was taught to make tortillas, clean the house, do the laundry, and not associate with anyone outside the house. Associating with other people only allowed us to pick up undesirable habits. I guessed that this was the reason that I was not allowed to be as social with my friends as I had wished. When my friends would ask me to sleep over at their house, my grandma would ask, "Why? You don't have a bed here?" She could not un-derstand any need for friendship.

From all of the stories I had heard about my great grandmother Maria, she reminded me of Sybil's mother. That girl had 16 personalities. I remember seeing the movie with Sally Field and Joann Woodward. They would have flashbacks of Sybil's mother tying her up in the kitchen and beating her up in the living room. This was my great grandmother. She was a monster. She used to say that if she knew which of her veins the Spanish blood coursed through, she would cut her skin and watch the blood drip to the ground. I started feeling the same way about the Mexican blood that coursed through my own veins.

My grandma still tells me today how she wonders what her mother Maria would think of me and my "ways." As a child, I didn't want to cook, sew, clean, and stay home everyday. That kind of life was like prison, and I did everything I could to escape. My grandmother has called me an Oreo since I was a young girl, you know, brown on the outside, white on the inside.

The women in my family seemed to be a part of some weird military. Everyday is the same. You get up at the same time every morning. You eat at eleven and four, and you can snack at night if you want. You bathe on certain days, go to the grocery store on certain days. Every conceivable action has a specific time and place, and there are few good reasons to change it. My grandma was miserable. Why would I want to work so hard in order to be miserable?

Through my "training," I learned that Mexican girls worked their asses off so they could get married, have kids, make a lot of food, and then have no one to eat it with. When you serve others, they eat before you. Mexican men were usually drunks, with shiny hair and a cross around their necks. They married you so they could eat well and dedicated their lives to making your life a living hell.

*Performer walks to center stage.*
It seemed to me that whiteness was my only choice. So I ran to it.
At 10 years old I accepted whiteness into my heart
At 15 I had a personal relationship with it.
At 20, three white men had already asked for my hand. And, one of them was even a Baptist.
I no longer exhibited symptoms of being Mexican.
I didn't speak the language.
I didn't know how to cook the food.
I couldn't keep things clean or orderly.
I did not have what it took to run a household.
People would ask me all the time what I was.
They always thought I was Italian or Greek.
And I took pride in that. I was glad that it wasn't obvious.

I was Mexican, but not really Mexican.

As I grew older, I would look at other Mexican girls and wonder what is was like to be them. They had long dark hair, thick skin, and an accent to match. They all seemed to be wearing the same cross on their chest—a cross I no longer believed in.

As I grew whiter, my grandmother would look at me, shake her head, and tell me how my mother would turn in her grave if she could see me now.

The Oreo. Brown on the outside, white on the inside.

My dad used to tell me that my mom always wanted me to marry a Mexican man—so not to taint the blood.

I wanted a nice white guy.

They had jobs, other than bussing tables.

They came home to their wives.

They didn't send money home to their mothers in Mexico.

I used to hear my family tell me what my mom would have wanted me to be.

But, what was I?

Last year I went to Kentucky for the weekend to visit some friends. While I was eating in a Mexican restaurant, I noticed that people were looking at me kind of funny. My friend informed me that people around there were not used to seeing brown people in town. I looked around to see which brown people he was talking about and discovered that he was talking about me.

I had become a white reflection. My reflection was so bright that it blinded me from seeing Gabriella's burned neck, my mother's dead body, my grandmother's servitude, and my own blood.

I think I know what my mom wanted me to come back to. And I'm on my way.

A few months ago I went on a date with a Mexican man. He's got thick, wavy dark hair and sometimes it looks shiny. Sometimes I stare at it without him noticing, and I remember the days when I said I would never date a Mexican man. When I walk into his house, I can feel my mom smile because she knows I am closer to home than I have ever been.

His house is very familiar to me. He has the lard canister right by the stove because we are always cooking, well, he is. I am not so good at it yet. But he is helping me. He has been taught to waste nothing, especially food.

He has the sequenced sombrero in the living room—just in case a Mariachi band shows up. It reminds me of the sombrero that hung in our house when my mom was alive. He has a set of maracas in his bedroom. The kind I used to have when I was five years old. Sometimes he tells me things in Spanish, and even though I don't understand what he says, it makes my heart pound. Something the white man has never done for me.

And I smile. Not as an Oreo, but as a Latina.

*Adrienne Viramontes and Her Mother*

*Adrienne's Communion*

## Chapter Four

# Dave Fanno: The Pit!

## Script Two: The Coke Plant

*I met Dave Fanno ten years before I would ever work with him on his series of descriptive narratives, which might be considered performative creative non-fiction. Fanno was an undergraduate in my oral interpretation class. For his final assignment in the class, he wrote about his experience of being in prison. The text was well written, desperate, and engaging. I seldom saw him after this undergraduate class. He took a job as a journalist for a local newspaper. By the time he returned to graduate school, Fanno had developed as a journalist, having won an award for his article about driving the speed limit.*

*Although he was a respected professional, I thought of him as the individual who wanted to transcend his background. We shared an ethnic identity as working-class Italian Americans and a similar sense of humor and cynicism.*

*In the course of being in the graduate program, Fanno began to talk openly about a period of his life that caused him great pain—the period of working in the coke plant at a northwest Indiana steel mill. His work at the coke plant was tied to his identity as the grandson of working class immigrants. The coke plant became a metaphor for Fanno and his family's struggle to fit into American culture. A coke plant is the basement of the steel mill where the working conditions are grueling and inhumane.*

*Recognizing Fanno's descriptive journalistic style of writing, I encouraged him to write about his experiences of working in the steel mill. Prior to writing this text, we discussed Pietro DiDonato's story "Christ in Concrete." "Christ in Concrete" is about an Italian immigrant who gets buried alive in concrete while working on a New York bridge. The story reminds those of us who were children or grandchildren of immigrants that coming to America was a tragic experience. As children and grandchildren of immigrants, many of us feel the need to atone for the tragedies our ancestors experienced. Working in the coke plant was a form of atonement for Fanno.*

*"The Coke Plant," one in a series of narratives, is a piece of creative non-fiction that viscerally describes a day of working in the plant. As an autobiographical text and a personal narrative, Fanno performs "The Coke Plant" primarily through vocal performance choices, which complement the text.*

## THE COKE PLANT

"Alberts, Kenneth; Hatcher, Michael; Healy, James; Musselman, Joseph; Zahn, Reginald. Board shuttle number two for the 76-inch mill, pronto. Cassidy, Kevin; Miller, Paul." The foreman continued to bark out the names of the next generation of Inland Steel mill workers. "Rodriguez, Miguel; Schau, Walter; Thompson, Tim." We all stood in clusters around the shuttle buses that would transport us to the plant locations for the first day of work and what turned out to be a day to pick up mill clothes, safety gear, and a locker number to store our belongings. Some of the new hires were headed to sites to begin apprenticeships because they had checked off the boxes on their applications marked "electrician," "pipe fitter," "mechanical," or other skilled positions. And of course I stood among those who checked off the box marked "general labor" because I really had no ambition to learn a trade or a skill. I was happy with a ten-dollar an hour job. I was 18. Why the hell should I learn a skill?

I was among those who were headed to the No. 3 coke plant, one of three areas that my dad had warned me about. "Don't take a job in the blast furnace or the open hearth. And you definitely don't want to work in the coke plant. It's the dirtiest job in the entire mill." "FAHno, David," mispronounced by the burly barker, but I knew who he meant. I boarded the shuttle behind six other new coke plant workers and there were five more behind me. There was a bounce in my step, and I could see the excitement on the faces of the others — 10 men and 2 women. We were going to be earning a king's ransom at $10-plus per hour and all the overtime you wanted. We were all close in age and, later I would discover, we were all single and looking forward to those big paydays. We weren't worried about the dirt, the shift-work, or the irrepressible heat from the coke ovens. We were on our way to fat paychecks and working-class status.

The coke plant shuttle stopped in front of a dirty, red brick building. Soot that escaped from the battery ovens had settled onto the walls over decades, and the wind and sun had done their parts to burn and bake the grit into the bricks. I jumped off the shuttle and followed the group in through the double-glass doors. We were led into a lunchroom and told to grab a seat on the benches until a foreman arrived. All the new recruits were given slips of paper the size of a receipt like the ones from dry cleaners. The receipt had shirt and pant size, shoe size, and hat size. We handed those receipts to some guy who stood behind a counter and in front of long, deep, and high rows of shelves in a clothing store for steel mill "active wear." Each time he snatched a receipt from a new recruit's hand, the guy would disappear between the narrow rows of wooden shelves in the dimly lit back of the room. I tried following him with my eyes a few times, but he seemed to disappear in the dark and then suddenly reappear in another spot behind the counter with a stack of issued gear. The scene was exactly like those old Army recruiting movies. I was issued my "greens." That's the official term for Inland Steel's plant uniform. Greens are heavy canvas flame retardant clothing worn over long underwear, essentially a jacket and pair of pants. Regardless of the outside temperature, coke plant employees (at least the grunts or laborers) wore long underwear underneath their plant clothing all year to protect their skin, or essentially their asses. The temperature could be a sweltering 90 degrees in the middle of July with humidity pushing the barometer to 100 percent, and we were required to wear the "long-johns."

I was given a black pair of metatarsals, 12-pound steel-toed ankle high boots with an additional flap of steel that covered the laces I had ordered during the screening session with the personnel office one week earlier. Other essential items included:

- A canvas pair of wristlets, a foot-long sock-type piece of clothing that wrapped around the end of the jacket's green sleeves (no puns please) to protect against any hot coal slipping into the sleeve.
- A pair of heavy suede steel mill gloves with extended canvas ends to overlap the wristlets.
- A pair of Buddy Holly black safety glasses with wire mesh sidepieces.
- A flannel-lined, red and green (very Italian) flame retardant skull cap to wear inside the safety helmet, and
- An eight-pound safety helmet with two pieces of white tape across the top from side to side and back to front. The X indicated a new recruit, or in my mind, a target for everyone. Recruits were also given a heat shield that attached to the front of the safety helmet. Heat shields were to be flipped down if you were working in an area with an open flame. Safety, safety, safety, and the mill protecting its ass.

The first week was an introduction to the new environment. Fellow workers were helpful, foremen were considerate and patient, and nearly everyone I encountered seemed relatively happy to be working at this money factory. It was like that every day for the first month. The locker room for dressing on the day shift was clean (for a steel mill, about as clean as an old high school locker room). We'd work for two hours and then take a 20-minute break, which usually meant walking back to the lunchroom, another five minutes from the work site. We had two breaks each shift, plus a lunch break in a very clean lunchroom with vending machines. The work was all labor: sweeping, shoveling, digging, moving, and cleaning. Nothing was complicated or difficult. After our shifts, we'd return to the locker room for a "cleansing" shower. I drove out of the plant parking lot at 3:10 in the afternoon each day wondering what to do with the next eight hours. My only responsibility was to be at the job and ready by 7 a.m., Monday through Friday. After an eight-hour shift, occasionally a sixteen-hour stay if overtime was offered, I'd use my time frivolously spending cash in bars or slipping quarters into pinball machines. I started thinking that maybe, just maybe, I could become comfortable with this routine. It didn't seem that bad. But, I hadn't considered what life was like in the plant on weekends and midnights and the dreaded three o'clock to eleven o'clock shift. My world changed with the introduction of shift work.

Shift work altered my sleeping cycles, my emotional stability, my sense of routine, and essentially my attitude about everything. I was a grunt steel worker: picking up paychecks every two weeks, paying some room and board money to my mom, and spending the rest of it on continually reliving my past and forgetting about the future. The job was a grind of physical pain: lifting forty heavy pounds of wet coke dust onto a two-foot wide shovel blade and flipping the slop onto a conveyor belt during back-to-back shifts; using a 10-foot steel rod to dig, prod and poke burning coal from a 2,000 degree oven, trying to loosen the red-hot embers and start a lava-like avalanche; inhaling toxic fumes emitting from asbestos-lined ovens each day inside the coke plant; shoveling out tar spills from the inside of contained tanks (the fumes made me light-headed, once passing out into about five inches of tar and lying there for 25 minutes until a coworker found me). I remember thinking, "How in the hell did my grandfathers do this for 40 years? What drove my uncles to commit to this suffering? Why had my father decided that working in a steel mill was the best option for survival when in reality the mill was a morgue?" Plenty of room. No waiting. A wasteland of cast-off dreams and tin soldiers.

Christopher Columbus, an Italian, ventured oceans to discover new lands and new treasures in the late 15th century. A little more than 400 years later, the first generations of my family, more Italians, settled in North America and were introduced to a new world and new adventures. They searched for a future and found comfort nestled in the valleys of eastern Pennsylvania and in the rising landscape of Tennessee, possibly because it reminded them of the land they left, or maybe because it was the only available space. They were unskilled, yet they were determined to face unknown challenges. My mother's family decided to earn its living by tilling the land and raising crops. My father's family, like many Italians, was driven by the age of industrialization, factory work and steel mills, and maybe a few games of craps. During the era of the Great Depression, thousands of Americans were forced out of work, and out of their environments, and some out of their minds. My two grandfathers made the decision to look for work in another part of the country in an effort to change their fortunes and futures. Their families told them that moving to northwest Indiana, Hammond, and East Chicago specifically, was silly and dangerous without bona fide jobs, but they went regardless, those rebel sons.

As a child and a teen, I rarely heard a negative story about Inland Steel from my grandfathers. In fact, I heard funny stories about the daily events, stories about the pain and toil that "made you a man." Days at the blast furnace, the cold strip, the plant. Ah, the glory days. My dad hired in at Inland in 1953 at 18. When I turned 18, it was assumed that I'd be the next generation. My cousins and me. Why consider anything else, right? If the steel mill was good enough for our fathers and our grandfathers, then it was good enough for us. I kept thinking "40 years at one place of work. The steel mill. No stinkin' way." But history was ready to be created, and the future of American industry was moving away from heavy steel production. It was the late 1970s, the end of prosperity for thousands of workers in the steel mills. Those mills and lakeshore factories linked generations of families and produced an infinite number of stories. The mills drove the economy in northwest Indiana for 40-plus years, but the end was near.

I never actually wanted a job at the mills. I witnessed the physical and mental abuse in my grandfathers and in my dad that accompanies the dedication to the paycheck and the security of the income. Steelworkers were handsomely rewarded for their regular time, overtime, time-and-a-half, and double overtime with large checks, multiple health benefits, weeks of vacation, and a sense of long-term security. The paychecks delivered the ability to sign thirty-year home mortgages, to drive away from car dealerships with a showroom display, to straighten teeth with braces, to build a two-car garage, remodel a kitchen with new cabinets, buy a stove and a refrigerator, replace the worn living room carpeting and the aged bathroom fixtures. It was unthinkable to consider any other future, according to my father, his father, my mother's father, uncles, aunts, three cousins, and all the siblings and spouses that benefited from the savings and checking accounts built upon Inland's rock. Before the ink could dry on an Inland Steel contract, a Master Lock representative secured your existence, someone else determining your freedom. I really wasn't ready to give up my freedom.

My intentions were to hire in at the "mill" and live with my parents for one year, save as much cash as possible, and head to the next location, yet to be determined. But, I hadn't seriously considered the seductive power of a healthy paycheck, especially when my bank account registered zero and what I owned wouldn't be collateral for a good pair of shoes. My father's advice was not to hire in at any of the coke plants. "It's the nastiest place out there and it's some of the toughest work. If they give you any choices, stay away from the coke plant." I heard the words, but I didn't truly listen. The next day, I was sitting in a room full of new hires, and I distinctly heard the personnel director's words: "Number 3 Coke Plant, start Monday." I knew then that an adventure waited.

The first few weeks at the coke plant *were* an adventure. I had seen those smokestacks rising out of the shoreline horizon, and I had watched those stacks purge black and gray into the blue sky. Those colors never blended well in my eyes. But now, I was on the inside and getting a close-up look at how that smoke invaded the sky. On dreary, rain-soaked, and foggy days, the iron structured metropolis menaced Lake Michigan's shoreline. Smoked bellowed from stacks, oozed from cracks in the concrete, and spilled black and white into the gray horizon. During storms, when thunder erupted and lightening split the haunted background, it was difficult to press onward. Even the lure of a fat paycheck wasn't enough. Even on sunny, blue-skied afternoons, Inland rose above the skyline shearing the clouds and blotting out the sun. It was a struggle to convince myself that the effort would pay off in the very near future, and the urge to reward myself for punching into purgatory daily was overwhelming.

The economic recession of the late 1970s was disassembling the steel industry one nut and bolt at a time. Layoff lists were posted in lunchrooms and office hall bulletin boards throughout the steel mill. Workers checked the lists weekly at first, but once the bloodletting began and the unemployment line doubled in length, workers flocked to the layoff lists daily and eventually hourly. My time in purgatory was short, but again I was letting everything and everybody control my destiny. Could I save a month of paychecks? Would I last that long avoiding the layoff list? Like the industry, stability and security were crumbling. The roaming souls looked lost. What would happen to us if we didn't have a steel mill to frequent? I focused on work and acquiring as much overtime and wealth as I could accumulate during the next thirty days, or until my gate pass was refused by security. It was a thirty-day stretch I had never previously experienced and that I'll never forget.

I was working the third shift, midnight to seven in the morning, in the middle of December during one of the coldest winters on record in the Midwest. I arrived on the job between 11:30 and 11:45 and began to prepare for my shift in the cavern known as the locker rooms under the coke batteries, at least at the Number 3.

I descended down eighteen to twenty steps of a dimly lit stairwell. There were two incandescent light bulbs encased in steel mesh and covered with years of coke dust near the top and bottom of the stairwell, but often only one bulb was lit. The stairwell walls and handrails were smothered with black soot, coke dust. Every ten minutes a fresh coat was sprinkled through the cracks in the ceiling, and as it settled onto the steps I'd grind another sole-full into the concrete. It crunched and burrowed into the cement, permanently grinding into the structure. I continued my descent and listened to the clanging echo of overhead heavy machinery rattling into the cavern below. I could see the dust flitter down from the ceiling and settle onto the tops of lockers and drop through the holes and vents contaminating anything inside the locker. The dust settled on the benches between the lockers. The black soot was everywhere, and I could smell the carbon odor. I was confident that it penetrated every pore and opening of my body. It always took three days to work the coke dust out of my body, evident in the remains of white Kleenex as I blew my nose or spit to clear my throat.

Rarely are pleasantries shared among co-workers preparing or finishing their shifts. The Number 3 lacks luxury, energy, spirit, and cleanliness, worse than a men's bathroom at a 24-hour truck stop cafeteria in the middle of Montana. As I stepped up to my locker and touched the dial on the combination lock, I could feel the grit of the coke dust on my fingertips as I twisted the dial right, left, right. It pushed itself into my pores and began to pollute my bloodstream. Welcome to work!

If I was smart enough to remember to buy a newspaper, I'd at least have clean print to stand on as I disrobed; otherwise, I'd search for a piece of anything that could separate my feet from the floor until I could slip into my metatarsals. After I had stripped down to my birthday suit and neatly packed my street clothes into a gym bag, I reached into my locker and removed the stiff long underwear, required for working on the battery. The underwear was stiff, seemingly over-starched, because I had lost eight pounds of sweat and water on yesterday's shift and the salt from my pores froze the underwear into a perpetual hook-hung state as it dried in my locker. I CRAWLED into the long underwear, feeling it scratch and pull at my skin like sandpaper. At least I had remembered to bring a fresh pair of cotton tube socks and a pair of wool socks to slip over the cotton socks. Every laborer would double-up on all of his clothing. I stood in the middle of the locker room looking like an extra from a Beverly Hillbillies episode. Time for your greens.

Inland generously washed the greens and provided us with a clean set, usually three pairs, during a week. But coke plant workers are last on the list, and if other workers were taking greens home and not returning them, or someone was using them as resale clothing in a corner shop, the plant ran short of greens, meaning it was my responsibility to clean the coke dust out of my clothing. Where are the industrial Laundromats?

I was working on my last shift for the week and only had a dirty pair of greens to cover my salt-infested long underwear. It felt as if I'd donned a suit of armor and was prepared to slay the battery dragon. A few more items and I'd be ready for the shift; metatarsals, canvas wristlets, suede gloves, flannel-lined skullcap, my severely scratched Buddy Holly black safety glasses, and that skull-protecting helmet. I'd removed the 'X' several months earlier. I was now prepared for ascension into purgatory!

I reported to the foreman on the Number 3 battery, and he gave me the instructions that I dreaded as part of the assignments at the coke plant. Not that any duty was inviting, but there were a few that were better than others. "Fanno, report to the cooling station. You'll probably be working in the pit tonight, and I don't think you'll have any help." The PIT! The word alone paints a negative portrait. That's where I'd be working for the next eight hours. The outside temperature was below zero. The only advantage in the pit was I'd be warm; wet, but warm. The pit was an enclosed portion of the cooling station, underground at the bottom of a conveyer belt that moved chunks of wet, cooling coal along miles of belt to a blast furnace. The coal was used in exactly the same manner that charcoal is used in a grill. Coal burned underneath blast furnace kettles to melt steel.

Tons of coke dust was shot into tall, narrow ovens on a coke battery. A battery usually had between thirty and forty ovens. Once the coke dust was dumped into an oven, the cooking process began to transform the particles of dust into huge chunks of coal used in the heating process of steel. After a twelve-hour cooking period, the cooked coke was pushed out of its oven into an open-top rail car. The rail car was pushed under a water station and gallons of water were dumped on the coal to cool the chunks. Once the chunks were sufficiently cool, a rail car was pushed to a cooling station and dumped on its side to spill the coal onto a conveyer belt system. Some of the coal would still need heavy watering as it smoldered on the rubber conveyer belt. A worker, hose-man, was given the responsibility of watering the burning and sometimes red-hot coal. If the coal burned through the conveyer belt, the entire production line stopped and created a huge backup. As the hose-man shot water onto the coal, tiny particles would break off and wash backwards down the conveyer belt into an area called "the pit." Those tiny particles fell off the end of the belt and created a continually growing pile of wet, thick sludge. If the sludge pile grew too high, it could also ruin the belt from friction created as the pile shoved against the belt. So, another worker was given the responsibility of removing the sludge by shoveling it back onto the belt; which was the only way out of the pit excluding a wall-mounted, eight-step, iron-rung ladder.

I descended into the pit. The heat from the coal and the tight area in the pit kept the temperature slightly above freezing; 40 degrees for the next eight hours. I stepped into the muddy, sludge-filled bottom of the pit, picked up the coal shovel standing against one corner, began chipping into the pile of sludge, and flipped a bladeful onto the conveyer belt. The pit was lit with a fluorescent fixture in an area the size of a walk-in closet, or a small bathroom. The walls were constantly wet from humidity, steam, and spray from the hose-man above. So, if I leaned against the wall to take a break, my back would be damp. I avoided leaning for the first couple of hours. I could take a fifteen-minute break every two hours, and, if I had a partner helping me on a particular assignment, I could relax more frequently as we helped each other keep our sanity. I was alone in the pit on this particular midnight, which gave me very little time for taking breathers. The conveyer belt rarely stopped, and neither did the falling particles of coal. Picking up the shovel blades full of wet coal dust was like picking up a shovel full of wet snow. The weight pulled at the muscles in my biceps, triceps, forearms, back, hamstrings, calves, ass, shoulders, neck, and temples. Could I do it for eight hours? Could I do it with a sixteen-pound steel shovel with a blade twice the size of a gardening spade?

After two hours of bending, jabbing the blade into the pile of sludge, extracting, raising, straining, and flipping, the cold and wet wall transformed into a pillowy-soft sofa. I didn't care how wet my back would be because I was soaked to the bone with sweat and water splashing off the belt. I had been standing in wet sludge, and my boots were frozen from the wet, cold and steel-toed inserts. My feet were frozen, and my head had a steady stream of sweat pouring into my eyes. I was constantly taking off the safety glasses to wipe away the humidity and fog. Frustrated with the continual wiping of my glasses and tired of readjusting my helmet, I tucked the glasses into my jacket pocket and removed the helmet and hung it from my belt. Two hours later, relief shouted down into the pit, "Fanno, take fifteen, but don't be fuckin' me around and get lost somewhere. I'll come lookin' for your ass if you're not back here in fifteen."

The warmth of the hose station lunchroom was inviting, but I really didn't want to sit because I was soaked. So, I grabbed my lunch, took a glance at my grubby, dirty hands, and considered washing them. That would have been too much effort. There were two other workers on their break, but none of us cared to converse. It was a cold night in December, I was working a lousy job, I was tired, hungry, and had only a few more minutes until my break was over, and layoffs were imminent. Merry Christmas!

I took a few extra minutes to try and dry off, but my relief made sure it was short-lived. As he came into the room, I asked if the belt was stopped and he shook his head. That meant he had walked away from the pile that was now building. If I had waited any longer, I could be digging for days. Back to "THE PIT!" Back to the wet walls, the steamy and cloudy atmosphere, the wet sludge bottom, the strain, the pain, the mindless numbing.

When the shift ended, I returned to the locker room mulling over how many more nights in the pit I could tolerate. Mulling over how many nights inside the Number 3 I could tolerate. The time spent on the battery, in the battery, and under the battery for eighteen months had been permanently etched into my body and had bored through my being. During the last eighteen months, I'd witnessed (and participated) in mentally and physically abusing my body. Had the paycheck kept me hypnotized, or had the lackadaisical lifestyle of a drifter kept me institutionalized? Maybe there was something else that I hadn't considered. At the end of my shift, I began to make a commitment to a change. As I drove away that morning, I thought about other avenues of making a living and new challenges. I looked into my rearview mirror as I headed south on Cline Avenue away from the mill and watched the sun rise above the smokestack horizon. It was burning off the morning frost on my windows and cutting through the black and gray smoke from the stacks.

## Chapter Five

# Jennifer Bianchi: I Was Terrified

## *Script Three: A Letter To Sam*

*Jennifer Bianchi entered my office with her dog, Hannah. Hannah, a large retriever mix, looked at me with fear. No doubt, she took me for the new vet, who was about to examine her. I went to the small refrigerator I keep in my office and pulled out a turkey sandwich. I gave Hannah half of the sandwich, which she ate, hesitantly at first, but with far more confidence a few moments later. "I know you wanted to meet her," Bianchi laughed. I thanked her for introducing me to Hannah. In the time I had worked with Bianchi on her script, "A Letter to Sam," I had had the opportunity to meet her family members—all except Hannah.*

*Bianchi's first foray into the study of single motherhood began with a paper she authored which examined media depictions of black versus white single mothers. She handed in a thoughtful analysis, which demonstrated how being a single mother carries a stigma. In a course I taught entitled, "Theories of Oral Interpretation," Bianchi began to collect narratives of single motherhood. We talked about her project, and she began seeking single mothers to interview. However, she was drawn back to her family, realizing that her mother, grandmother, and aunt were all single mothers. Coming from this lineage of single mothers was an enormous component of Bianchi's identity. Her primary narrative is about being raised in the cultural context of single mothers. She began to build a script with these family narratives. In her original script, the single mothers spoke to one another about their experiences. But the talking back and forth subtracted from the original narratives. To preserve them, Bianchi edited them and performed them as a collection of her family narratives about single motherhood. By studying the narratives line by line, Bianchi determined which lines were unnecessary or disconnected from the entire piece. The edits preserved the original narratives but gave a feeling of cohesiveness to each narrative.*

*I suggested that the collection was not complete without Bianchi's own narrative. As she built in her narrative, Bianchi decided to call this collection, "A Letter to Sam." She wanted the performance to be a familial artifact that would assist her son in his life. When she made this commitment to complete the text for her son, Bianchi felt a strong desire to create a performance event. Initially, she thought of casting different individuals for the four narratives but then decided she would like to embody the narratives.*

*The show opens with Bianchi reading the first part of her letter to her son. She introduces each narrative with a collage of photos and music that best represent the character which she will embody. After embodying the four women, including herself, Bianchi concludes with the textual display of the letter on a screen for the audience to read and a final photo of her and her son. While her intention was to create a tribute to her family, the script is a letter of pride written to all single women.*

## A LETTER TO SAM: FAMILY NARRATIVES ON SINGLE MOTHERHOOD

*The following letter appears on screen for the audience to read.*

Samuel,

My reasons for writing you are countless. You are my son and I am eternally in love with you. Your big bright eyes, the smell of your hair, the rasp in your young voice when you whisper in my ear. *You* are *the* most important to me, which is exactly why this letter is for you. Besides, there are many pieces of my life that I want you to know, to recognize, and that I want you to love . . . because I am your mother. Someday, you'll question me and not understand who I am, but through this letter, and many more to come, you will learn my strongest desires, my heartaches, my pleasures, and my where my heart is. And through this letter, you will know your home, your family, and yourself. Although you are very young, you will soon appreciate these things I am about to write.

It is so very important to me that you know where you come from . . . the family that embraces you, and the people who love you deeply. As you can already see, the majority of our family are women. You are the first boy to be brought into the family in over 25 years. Because of this, you should know who these women really are because they are your foundation, your home, and they are deep in your heart. These amazing women, your great-grandmother Helen, your aunt Lisa, your grandmother Deborah, are undoubtedly the most influential in my life. Without them, I wouldn't know my world as I know it today. They have taught me responsibility, loyalty, individuality, independence, unity, love, and

most importantly, how to be the best mother to you. I have put together a "story," if you will, that illuminates these beautiful women in my world.
Love, your mother

*Photo of Sam appears, fades, then a collage of photos from Helen's life appear on the screen. As the collage ends, Helen walks to stage holding a coffee cup with Sam's photo. She is a mentally sharp woman in her late 60's. She sits down at a table and begins her narrative.*

A five-letter word for "the state of being one." (shows the audience scribbling on a crossword puzzle). That little shit! He's always got a marker in his hands. Little shit! But those sweet hands. I've always loved the hands of children. So busy, and curious, so innocent and unknowing . . . and always marking up something they shouldn't be touching. Sam is my first great grandson. He calls me "Baba." It would be nice if Rich were here.

I remember my last night with Rich. I kissed him and said, "Goodnight, Rich. I love you." And he said, "I love you, too." That was his last breath. He was gone. My husband Rich died in 1986 from a stroke. The last one finally took him. He had been sick for a while, but he stayed home . . . and walked a lot to stay healthy. (pause) But sure enough, I would catch him smoking. Halfway down the block, I'd see a puff of smoke floating behind him. Ha . . . He thought he was so sneaky. You can't hide from your wife after 36 years.

It never occurred to me that I would become a single mother. When my husband died, Joey, the youngest of my children, was still in high school. But raising Joey had already been done. He just needed to be educated. Raising children, or parenting them, involves taking them to the doctor when necessary, making sure they behave, teaching them manners, getting them dressed and off to school, and going through all of those phases of childhood. I wasn't parenting Joey . . . I already had.

I never considered myself as a single mother because people saw me as a widow. Most single mothers have to deal with change. They move, change homes, or begin work, or the siblings split up. And they have to make that change smooth and comforting for the children. Rich passed away but we never deviated from our normal way of life. There was no changing houses or changing environments. Everything stayed the same . . . we stayed at home and we stayed together. But I realized that I needed to go back to work. A part-time job was offered to me, so I took it. It was the best I did for myself. It was also the first time I had no restrictions. I could come and go as I please, and after being married for 36 years, that was a challenge.

I feel very sorry for single mothers. I think that they have a hard road if they are *truly* parenting their children. I don't mean single mothers that are all over the damn place, leaving their children with sitters. But if they are truly parenting . . . then it is going to be hard. Financially it's hard because they don't have the money, and picking the right job is even harder because of other limitations. Who's going to stay home when one gets sick, or help them with their homework, talk to them as they go through life? Parenting is a 24-hour job and there aren't many breaks. As a single mother, you are mother, father, teacher, doctor, cab driver . . . you become everything to the kids. It's difficult to find work that lets you be all of those things. I feel for them. In this world, I think that most of us now have single mothers in their families. When I see these women who have to raise children, my heart goes out to them, I feel sorry for them because they lack that family unity; they lack some type of family traditions. And the children will eventually lack it. But it is good if they have supportive family around . . . grandparents, aunts, and uncles. I have always been so proud of my family.

I was fortunate to have and work on a relationship that was equal in all areas. People would say, "Oh, you were so lucky to have such a great relationship." It had nothing to do with luck. It worked because we made it work . . . *we* put forth the effort, constantly. You don't see that much in families these days. Things get difficult and people leave or split up. It is not fair for the children. We're adults and we need to think like ones . . . marriage is serious. It takes patience and understanding . . . and effort. I think that as a society, we don't look for permanent things any more. We look for what satisfies us at that time . . . and then when we are satisfied, we move on to the next. We have become a very temporary society . . . we need to renew our permanence to keep that unity.

Ha . . . I've found my five-letter word . . . U-N-I-T-Y. (pause) I could have never done it without my husband.

*Helen exits and a collage of photos of Lisa appear on the screen. When the collage finishes, Lisa enters carrying a basket of laundry. She is in her mid-30's.*

C'mon girls! Tub's full. Get in. Make sure Sam takes his socks off *before* getting in. Every time he's over he's gotta take a bath. "Kuma, can I take a bath?" he asks. Kuma, that's Croatian for Godmother. I'm also his favorite aunt. "Yah mom . . . I'll do it"

Here I am . . . back at home and going through my second divorce from the same man. I should have known it the first time around . . . ya know, that things wouldn't be any different. I don't understand sometimes why the hell I did it again? I know why . . . I wanted more children. I wanted them all to have the same father. Too many families have children that have different fathers, and I did not want to be one of them.

Lauren, my first daughter, was born in 1984, two years before my dad died. I was so in love . . . everything was going to be so awesome. We were going to be mommy and daddy, and it was going to be fantastic. We married when she was almost a year old. She was three when we divorced for the first time. After two years, we got back together. I wanted more children. I thought that the second time around was going to be different. Ya know, because *we* were different. It seemed like we grew up over two years. And there I was again, pregnant, for the second time. And then a third time . . . and then we married again.

We met at the Crown Point Courthouse to vow ourselves to each other . . . again. Romantic, huh? We *met* at the courthouse. We did not drive together. He took his lunch break while I got a sitter. And that judge that married us . . . I couldn't stop staring at him . . . he was so cute. Makes me laugh when I think about it, and sick . . . I can still feel that pit in my stomach eating at me when I think of how wrong things were. Who the hell *meets* at the courthouse to get married? And so we vowed ourselves to each other for the second time.

It took six years, three kids, and a thousand lonely nights before I changed my mind again. I guess some people got their limits. Nothing changed. I remember this one time when I was eight months pregnant, Lauren was eight, and Kelsey was one, and I needed something from the grocery store . . . milk or eggs or something like that. My husband walked in from work and before he could take his shoes off, I asked if he could run to the store. He looked at me with this disgusted look in his eyes. He has that look a lot, like he hates life and the people in it. He said to me, "Well, I worked all day, go get it yourself. Besides, what do you do all day besides take care of the kids." Ten minutes later, I am standing in the aisle . . . sweaty, big as a house with a one year old on my hip and an eight year old next to me. I just wanted a few things . . . not to stock the fucking house. I just kept thinking to myself, "I can't believe this. What am I doing? This is so not right."

But that's how it was. I always did things for the children and myself on my own. After a while, I just figured that I would be much happier if there wasn't such a hateful husband to come home to. I had to leave him for my own sanity. Ya know, when you are married, and you find yourself doing things . . . *all* the things . . . on your own, you finally tell yourself that this is not the way marriage is supposed to be. Marriage is supposed to be a journey together. I'm totally certain that I made the right choice leaving again because I'm happy. Of course I knew that it would throw me into a position of being a single mother, as if I wasn't already. I welcomed it . . . I couldn't wait.

Making decisions for my children has always come naturally, but it's a challenge. What to do or not to do in front of them, say or not to say. But sometimes you don't realize that the decision is right until a while after. I was talking with my oldest daughter last night . . . that happens more since she is getting older. She's not a kid anymore. So anyways, she said, "Mom, I think that we get along very well. We have a really good relationship." I thought, well yah. She continued on with a story about her friends and how they fight with their parents . . . actually fight . . . with slaps, and fists, and slamming doors. Then she turned to me and said, "I just think of how glad I am that we don't fight like that." And I thought, "Oh, how awesome that everything I have been doing with her whole life is really kind of making sense." She knows she can talk to me . . . always. So, sometimes you don't get immediate results when making decisions. As a mother, single or not, you just have to trust your instincts.

(calling) No. I'll wash your hair. I'll be there in a minute!

Our daily lives have changed so much. There are new dynamics of being a single mother . . . it's kind of a shock. When I was married, all I did was indulge myself in my kids' lives whereas now, I am breaking into my own life . . . without the security blanket of a marriage. I forgot to give them money for lunch one time, and I felt awful, or instead of picking them up for school, they sometimes come home to an empty house. But we deal and move on to the next day.

And people would say, "Oh, you have kids . . . are you married?" I would say, "No." They would condescendingly say, "Oh . . . divorced. Right?" I would get so pissed and think, " . . . and your problem is???" Too late, I don't like them anymore. You know, being a single mother is the biggest part of me. If I am ever going to have a relationship with anybody . . . intimate or not, they would have to know that I am a single mom. If they didn't like my situation or if they didn't want to be a part of it, then, I wouldn't want to be a part of them. I couldn't be their friend. I just don't care much of what others think of me. I am happy now.

Alright, I'm coming! Yah mom . . . I know

*Lisa exits and a collage of photos of Deborah appear on the screen. When the collage is finished, Deborah enters, carrying beach paraphernalia such as sun tan lotion, towel, beach chair. She is in her 50's, impatient and independent.*

Just when you take a turn called marriage, you realize it's the wrong turn. But, hey, they say you can recover from mistakes, right? We were married for five years. I loved him. I thought it would last for years more. We'd have a tri-level in Highland, a pool in the backyard, and a two-and-a-half-car garage.

By this time, I would have five more children and all of the neighborhood kids would come over and play. Well, there's no big house in Highland, or pool, or five other children. Why? Well, because I found myself with a cheating husband who had other children with another woman. I know I sound a bit bitter about this, but it turned out for the best. I'd like to think that adverse conditions are good for the soul. I thank him for forcing me to think about my life and where it was heading. Hey, when somebody goes out for a half gallon of milk and they don't come back for three days . . . you kinda do sit in corners and wonder where you are. Have I left and come back and not known it? Where is that fucking milk . . . am I still here waiting for my goddamn milk? Where the hell is he? "I think it's breakdown time . . . NO!! Not now," I told myself. "I have to move on" . . . I had to raise my daughter and think ahead. I needed to break myself of a pattern that would head me down the wrong road. So I got a good job. Everything changed.

There I was . . . Single, with a two-year-old child to raise. I did not want to go back home and live. It was scary. I didn't know if I could make enough money or how I was going to make this situation work. Lucky for me, it was the beginning of women going to work. It wasn't so much the "in" thing to do, but other women were doing it and I didn't feel so alone. My mother once said to me, "Ya know, Deborah, you just have to remember that you are nothing but a statistic." Those were wise words. Becoming a single mother after marriage . . . Yep, it was a statistic, and it sounds so cruel to say, but it's not because you could play it both ways. I mean, it's sad that society has gotten to a point where it thinks that the breaking up of a family is a statistic, yet, it is good that it has gotten to that point because it doesn't . . . um . . . stigmatize as much. Ya know, people were judging but people were also taking a different stance on it. The ones that kept their husbands thought, "Did you fail, did he fail? Are you as good as the rest of us because we kept our husbands and our homes?" The ones that were getting divorced didn't feel so alone . . . but they did . . . becoming a statistic was a harsh reality check. But it gave strength. Smart, self-sufficient, hard working, and a caring mother was my new label . . . not a divorced, single parent . . . even though that was true. Us women had to strive for change . . . not be a victim of it. It was time to face your self worth. I used to think that I should have stayed with your father. Then I think, "Fuck no." That's not the answer. I think that as a single parent, in my day, you just had to try harder so you weren't considered trash or poor or fucked up.

I thought I'd get married again and as time went on, it was obvious that I wouldn't. So instead of *hoping* for another marriage, or *hoping* for another man, or *hoping* for more children, I just took advantage of what *was*. And have the best time with it. In that respect, I did not give a shit what anybody thought. In fact I used to think that a couple were a tad bit jealous because I was doing what I wanted to do. But there were a lot of other people's opinions that I cared about. People would judge me because I was an "apartment owner" instead of a "home owner." People in my day would single divorced women out and say things like, "that kid from the divorced family," or "that kid from the broken home."

My generation was the beginning of this single motherhood stuff. I didn't want my daughter to do anything because of my situation. It was never her cross to bear. If people were going to judge us . . . I wanted them to judge me — not her. Hell, I didn't even want them to judge me because there were times I didn't want to tell people that I was coat-checking on a Saturday night for extra cash.

I remember one year at work when I received a bonus, my daughter was seven . . . and it put gifts under the tree. It was a tough year, but it worked out. Ya know, I don't know how it happened, but everything always seemed to be there when I needed it. Sometimes I can't figure out if I am looking out for myself or if someone's looking out for me. I can't analyze myself that much anymore, but it has always worked out . . . and I think that's a miracle. It's a balance.

*Deborah exits and a collage of photos of Jennifer appear on the screen. When the collage is finished, Jennifer enters.*

On November 4, 1998, my son, Samuel, was born. I stared into those little blue eyes for what seemed like a lifetime . . . then he finally looked back at me. (pause) And at that point I realized I was a mother. I was terrified. I know it sounds so cliché, but having a baby is a hell of a lot easier than being a mother. I could feel my life change while holding him in my arms. So what the hell am I going to do when I get out of here? So many decisions, so many choices. And staying single was the best choice I made.

The biggest fear at that point in my life was being in a marriage for the wrong reasons. And being pregnant everyone would ask . . . when's the wedding? Eventually, I felt myself back away from marriage, so much that people still think that I am afraid of marriage. I'm not . . . I'm really afraid of divorce. Being around divorce makes you wonder why people jump into marriages, and then jump out. If you make that decision, live with it. Divorce isn't always a remedy. It's more of an easy way out if you ask me. If you love someone, then you fucking make it work, you work hard at it, even when it drains your last ounce of energy. That's how I feel about my son. Even when days are draining, I still put every piece of me into it. And if I wasn't willing to do that in the first place, then I should have thought about that before I decided to have him. Sure, I never could have imagined the impact it would have on my life, or the challenges I would face, but I didn't head for the hills when I became afraid. And I remember the first time I was afraid. It was at my son's baptism, because for the first time, I felt judged. When Terence and I, that's Sam's father, met with the priest to go over the baptism *agenda,* he asked if we were married. When we told him that weren't, he explained that Sam wasn't allowed to be baptized during mass . . . it had to be after mass. Of course, we still had to attend mass. See, Father Jack was concerned that people would figure out our little secret. After 12 years of a Catholic school education, I know that baptism, by definition, is the welcoming of a new member into the community, the Christian community. After 20 minutes with Father Jack, I learned that being a single mother (pause) put me in back of church feeling unwelcome. After the baptism, which took place in a lovely private ceremony, I picked up my son, along with my pride, and celebrated with my family. And I still wonder to this day, what people must have thought as we sat in the back of the church watching all those babies being baptized. I guess it's easy to put someone else in the back of the church when you're the one afraid of being judged. Thank you Father Jack for today's lesson in guilt. I learned that being a single mother is something to be ashamed of.

So, everyday I sit and explore what more I want for my son and me. Why I want it. There are a million things I want for my son. I want him to be a good person. You know, I want him to understand who he is. I want us to talk, like my mother and I did. I want us to sit down every night and eat dinner together. Just because I am single, I never want my son to feel that I don't have time for him. Kids need reassurance about how to navigate through their lives, and if at any moment my son wants to talk about anything . . . All I care about is that my son knows that I will be waiting with an open heart. And just because I am not married doesn't mean that my child will not grow up with values or rules or traditions. It bothers me sometimes that single mothers are looked at as missing something . . . as if we have this void in our life just waiting to be filled. My mother once said to me, "Never compromise yourself." And that is exactly what I am doing. I am relentlessly searching for what my heart desires . . . and I'll teach my son the same. If that is not a value . . . you tell me what is.

*The following appears on the screen for the audience to read*

My dear Sam, you are my world. You are my son. Hopefully, through this story, you will understand me more completely, and understand the worlds that have touched you in so many ways. I have given my love to you for which you have given me the gift of motherhood. I wish you knowledge . . . I wish you power . . . I wish you inspiration . . . and most of all, I wish you love . . . because I love you.

Your mother

*A photo of Sam and Jennifer appears*

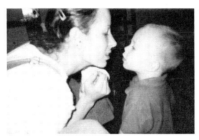

*Jennifer Bianchi and Her Son, Samuel*

# Chapter Six

# Erin Okamoto Protsman: The Child, The Flower, and The Rifle

## *Script Four: Excerpt from Without Due Process*

*Like all scripts intended for live performance, video documentaries demand creative attention. They can be composed of interviews carefully edited to create a rhetorical message, but also demand a message that is compelling and worthwhile. "Without Due Process" is based on one family's accounting of the Japanese internment, which originates from a story told to former graduate student Erin Okamoto Protsman. Okamato Protsman's family were interned in Poston, Arizona, and Manzinar, California, during World War II.*

*As a child, Okamoto Protsman interviewed an aunt about the internment for a school project. Her aunt told her a story of being interned and trying to pick some flowers located outside the barbed wire fence of the internment site. Her aunt, who was a child at the time, was met with a rifle in her face by an armed guard. The story haunted Okamoto Protsman because of the contrast between the act of picking flowers and the violent symbol of a gun. Because she framed her life around knowing that the internment deeply affected her family, the incarceration experienced by her family became Okamoto Protsman's primary narrative. She knew that such an event made a long-lasting impression on how cultural members interacted in American society. Thus, Okamoto Protsman created a documentary about her family's experience of the Japanese internment. In an effort to purge this painful experience from her family's memory, she interviewed all living family members about their experiences in the camps.*

*Documentary seems to be the most appropriate genre for these interviews/ narratives. By selecting this genre, the individuals who experienced this tragedy had the opportunity to present their story in their words. In so doing, "Without Due Process" yields insight into the Japanese American culture as well as to the internment.*

*Here is an excerpt from the beginning of the video:*

## EXCERPT FROM *WITHOUT DUE PROCESS*

"Without Due Process" chronicles the experiences of the Okamato family, who were incarcerated in internment camps during World War II. The video includes interviews with family members as they discuss their experiences before, during, and after being interned. In the following excerpt from the video, members describe and share how they learned about the internment:

## Beginning

> *Erin*: I just remember at a very young age being very proud that my family was Japanese American and that I was different because my family got to go to the relocation camps. I always knew it was unfair, and I knew the government was wrong because that's what I was taught, but I was very proud that they endured it. And my older brothers and my older sister said I should be very proud that grandma and grandpa and your dad and your aunts and uncles had to go through this, and they survived it.

> *Erin*: (As narrator) Americans united and patriotism soared during World War II. For Japanese Americans, however patriotic, life became a nightmare as their country turned against them because they resembled the Japanese enemy who attacked Pearl Harbor. Even though they were extremely loyal to the United States, over 120,000 people of Japanese ancestry were taken from their homes, stripped of their possessions, and herded into camps without due process. They lived behind armed guards and barbed wire for the duration of World War II. My family was among those whose loyalty was questioned. This is their story.

> *Chris Komai* (Japanese American National Museum curator): The exhibit "Common Ground: The Heart of the Community," holds an entire section about the WW II experience of Japanese Americans. It is significant to America in that 120,000 Americans of Japanese ancestry were forced by their own government to live in concentration camps in some of the most desolate parts of the United States. They were never tried. They were never charged. They never received due process. What's interesting is that many years later, Ronald Reagan signed the civil liberties act of 1988 providing for reparations and an official apology which sort of put an end to the cycle. Otherwise, the other parts of the WWII experience besides the mass incarceration have to do with the valiant military service of Japanese Americans in Europe and in the Pacific. The most famous of them are the 100th battalion and the 442nd regimental combat team, which was the most decorated unit for its size and in terms of its service. Lesser known but no less heroic were the work of Japanese Americans who served in the military intelligence service, many of them as code-breakers, interrogators, that sort of thing. All that story is compacted into parts of the exhibit, "Common Ground."

## Before the Evacuation

*Erin*: Before the mass incarceration of the Japanese Americans during WWII, my close-knit family members lived in southern California.

*Dorothy*: It was an idyllic life. We had this house with ten children, ten very vibrant, lively children. I was never lonely. I'm sure we were quite poor, but I never felt it because most of our friends were at the same level we were. We all went to the same church, the same schools. So, it was a very closely-knit community and everyone was there to help one another—a wonderful life.

*Excerpt from a letter written by General John DeWitt*: Particularly the Japanese. I have no confidence in their loyalty whatsoever . . . .In order to meet that threat, we have got to do two things. We have got to be able to enter their homes, and premises, search and seize immediately without waiting for normal processes of the law.

## The Evacuation

*Erin*: Without warning, my family was uprooted and sent to concentration camps located in the barren deserts of Poston, Arizona, Manzanar, California, and in the high plains of Heart Mountain, Wyoming. During this evacuation period, my family had to give up their possessions, their privacy, and their freedom.

*Dorothy*: I was about seven and a half or eight years old. All I know is that my parents were saying that the Japanese attacked Pearl Harbor, and we were suddenly identified as the treacherous Japanese enemy that spurred this attack. There were rumors that we would all be evacuated or moved into camps, and it certainly did come true.

*George*: Roosevelt issued an executive order and all Orientals in Washington, Oregon, California, had to move inland. If you had a chance, if you had the money, you could move inland and set up your own house, but you couldn't live on the West Coast. They posted signs on the telephone poles, in the papers, and radios. Instructions for us to follow. What the hell's happening because at least the schools you went to, they told us in history class, that can't be done. We had to move, and there was no due process or anything. They had to just move us. The MPs came in. They said, you can pack whatever you can carry. And they loaded us on buses. Off we went.

*Frank*: It was through the newspaper, radio, bulletins. They were pasted all over the telephone poles. The army put them up and said we were going to be evacuated at a certain date, at a certain time, and whatever you could pack, you could carry. We had to sell our car, our furnishings. That was the time I thought it was very unfair because people knew you had to move, and they weren't about to pay anything for your car. It was a give away. And I thought at that time that my father said we paid so much for the car, and we can only sell it for this. That was just part of the problems that we faced at that time.

*Roy*: After WWII started, it became very rough on us. We lived in the rural area of Santa Ana. We weren't allowed to go into Santa Ana. Everything was no Japs allowed. Signs were posted that said "No Japs Allowed." You just really felt it and the FBI would follow you. We had curfews. After 9pm, you couldn't be on the street. Sundays where you'd go to church for the evening, you had to be home by a certain time or the FBI was right there. There were killings after Japan attacked Pearl Harbor. People would get knocks on the door and someone would come there. Bam, just shoot them because they were Japanese. Stories like that—people were getting shot. So people wouldn't answer the door— "Don't answer the door until we find out." Whenever there was a knock on the door, no one answered until one of my parents went to the door.

*Taye*: I know my parents were concerned about how they would dispose of their possessions. We had a car. We didn't own our house. My dad had all of his gardening equipment to dispose of. I know eventually we sold everything at rock bottom prices. I think my mom was saying she had to sell her refrigerator for ten dollars, and my dad stored his gardening equipment at this building. He was doing gardening work for these people, but when he came back, it was gone.

*Dorothy*: We didn't have that much time. Signs were posted and we were all supposed to be corralled at a certain time and report to a certain station and the bus would pick us up. We could only take what we could carry, so of course, that meant that many of our treasured possessions would be left behind. Being practical—clothing and kitchen utensils were a priority. Most of our things were just left there. Lots of people took advantage of that and swooped down like vultures. Knocked on our doors and offered fifty dollars for our truck or ten dollars for our piano, knowing that we could not take it with us.

*George*: Thomas, me, Frank, Hannah, we packed just what we wore and maybe a change or two. The rest we packed for the little kids. The little kids had to have more than one set of clothes, so we packed a lot of their clothes.

*Taye*: I know we got up at the crack of dawn and I'm not sure how we got there, but we boarded these buses and being at such a tender age, I felt a sense of excitement. I thought it was one great adventure. We were on a convoy of buses, so as we rolled through the cities, people would line up to gape at us. Of course, I didn't know any better. I thought we were celebrities. I was enjoying myself, but as the day wore on, it got boring and tiring. They did give us box lunches, and I thought that was grand. And then, the convoy got lost. It took us ten hours. By the time we got there, it was a late hour.

*Masako*: (Roy's wife) Well, the area I'm from, we went to San Anita racetrack because we lived in Hollywood. Our family was too small to live in the stables.

The horse stables were bigger than the barracks they had built. So we got a barrack instead of a horse stable, and I remember standing in line and getting our shots. They had to innoculate you for different things.

*Taye*: It was terrible because we got there at a late hour, and I remember them handing us our bedding. Everyone got an army blanket. They gave us sacks that were to be filled with straw, and that was our mattress. Everything was barren. And it just hit me that we were going to be there for who knows how long. I remember crying myself to sleep at night.

*The Okamoto Family After the Internment*

## Chapter Seven

# Ami Kleminski: Cross-dressing to Survive

## Script Five: I Am Not Contained between My Boots and My Hat

*Autoethnography, which combines elements of autobiography with a study of a particular culture, allows the writer to create an inventive script based on the reflections on one's experience in the culture being represented. Ami Kleminski's autoethnography "I Am Not Contained between My Boots and My Hat" is an example of autoethnography as script. Using this genre to bring her day-to-day experiences to life, Kleminski contextualizes what it means to work as a female in a predominantly male trade. Kleminski explains how she had to cross-dress to survive in the steel industry. Using a combination of theory and experience, a technique commonly used in the creation of autoethnography, Kleminski self-reflexively locates herself in a steel culture, providing self-critique as well as cultural critique. Here is her script:*

### I AM NOT CONTAINED BETWEEN MY BOOTS AND MY HAT

### Admission

This is an authoethnography. Am I stating what I hope will become the obvious? Yes. Why am I doing so? Perhaps as a public, yet personal, admission of who I am. The park bench observer. The one who, despite an overwhelming amount of contradictory medical research, still finds drinking and smoking somehow romantic—one who switches back and forth between the proverbial bartender and patron. Neumann (1996) stated that, "As a term of textual analysis and as an orientation to textual production, *autoethnography* renames a familiar story of divided selves longing for a sense of place and stability in the fragments and discontinuity of modernity" (p. 173). I find his words somehow tragic and beautiful, and that is what I love most about hearing another person's words. It is that connection—that unparalleled feeling that someone out there understands you. (Truthfully, being an anal and over-organized lover of list making, and the like, I appreciate having a name for *this* alone.) I am also a quote person and will leave this with the words of the Danish physicist Niehls Bohr, "I will endeavor never to write more clearly than I think." So it follows that instead of proper headings, I will use the profound and/or appropriate words of others, rather than headings, to precede the divisions in ideas that I have deemed fitting.

"Everything in life is speaking in spite of its apparent silence." (Hazrat Inayat Khan)

Identity is a social construct. Something that is constructed, however, has the capability for change. It can be deconstructed, altered, etc.; therefore, identity is a malleable entity. This allows for a person to develop, perform and adapt throughout one's lifetime, almost as a Darwinian means of survival. According to Coover & Murphy (2000):

> Identities are formulated and maintained over time through interactions both mediated and unmediated, direct and indirect, interpersonal and intercultural. Communication, then, is integral to the ongoing negotiation of self, a process during which others define individuals as they, in turn, define and redefine themselves. Consequently, research on the self-concept and its role in communication must necessarily consider both the existing identities that comprise the overall self as well as the social contexts where individuals are situated. (p. 125)

Effectively, one is able to fashion an identity conducive to one's politics of location and the temporal space in which she finds herself. This is not to suggest that one forfeit one's identity for a new one, but that one adds to her identity a *vocabulary* to live and work alongside other people. This illustrates openness to the proverbial *other* or rather a way of developing understanding and showing respect for oneself and other people. Hall's research (as cited in West 1990) argued that the politics of representation are a valuable tool for the process of identity formation (p. 263). This essentially includes creating and sustaining an identity. How and under what circumstance a person would employ such tactics is a process. To reiterate, to thrive, one must adapt according to her politics of location and spatial location. It is here that the concept of cross-dressing becomes an indispensable tool. It allows one to get an insider's viewpoint, to become part of *the team* and to be accepted into the dominant group(s). In the proceeding paragraphs, I will illustrate the use of gender cross-dressing as an instrument I have used for nearly eight years at my place of employment. I will offer narratives to elucidate the processes necessary to one's politics of representation and will conclude by offering possible queries to further expand this area of interest, as well as to give my personal interpretation of such.

Anyone who grew up in Northwest Indiana knows AM Steel. Someone in the family or a close friend either works in or has retired from the place. This entire area was built as a result of the steel mills along Lake Michigan. Even those who only drive down the I 80–90 toll road traveling to Chicago or Michigan cannot miss the *monstrosity* on the lake, as AM Steel encompasses approximately 4,000 acres of lakefront property. My father worked at AM Steel for over 31 years, and my brother has worked there for many years, as did my friends' parents and grandparents. This place has truly helped to support generations. Knowing about a place and experiencing a place are two very different things, however. The formation of any identity is based on some distinct features: one's present and prime identity, one's politics of location and spatial considerations. Each individual has a master narrative shaped by key events that took place in that individual's life. These are things that one carries around with her always, as this narrative is very personal and unique to each individual. One's politics of location are developed from one's worldview and subsequent mode of processing information. Spatial considerations relate to the place and the people (and the history of both of these) in which an individual finds herself.

My master narrative includes two key gender-related parts. The first part is a distrust of men that stems from my relationship with my father. I must note that this should not suggest that I dislike men; my best friend is a man. What it does suggest, however, is my cautious behavior with the male gender as a whole. The second part is a fear of rejection and a need for validation from women. To make this more comprehensible, I will briefly mention that while my father is a good person, he should have never been married and had children, as work and friends were his priorities. In this case, it was rather unfortunate for me that I look exactly like him. Unconsciously, my mother had a way of treating me like my father and showing much more interest in my younger sibling. The sight of me was too much for her sometimes, and while I do not excuse this behavior, I do understand it and have been able to give it a place in my head so I can work with it, so to speak. What her behavior, and my assumptions about her behavior, created was a little girl and now a woman who is very concerned with how she is viewed/treated by other women. So to reiterate, my identity is predisposed to a distrust of men and need for validation/fear of rejection from women.

I was 22 years old, going to school (when I felt like it), and working part-time at the Pier 1 Imports in Lansing, Illinois. My father saw this *lack of direction* as an opportunity to give me a nudge in the right direction, so to speak. I always thought he was just afraid I wouldn't get out of school until I was thirty, and he would get stuck paying my rent and tuition until such time as I graduated. While he was right, I was not receptive to the idea of a *real* job—that is until I learned how much money I would be making. So I drove up to AM Steel's employment office on the west side of the plant for an interview and was scheduled for a basic English and math skills test. This was a miserable process as I felt (and for the most part was) educationally superior to the rest of the group. I found the test insulting to my intelligence and feared that this was just the beginning. After another few weeks of physical examinations and employee orientation, I was finally deemed ready for work. My friends began cracking jokes that it was like the movie *Flashdance*. Images of me dancing in leg warmers with sexy, slow motion hair flips as I took my helmet off flew through their heads. I, on the other hand, already knew that I was in for a completely different adventure.

"I am not contained between my hat and boots." (Walt Whitman)

My identity and my politics of location, in relation to my professional life, were quite a challenge with respect to spatial considerations. Since October 1996, I have been employed in a production and shipping area of AM Steel. I am primarily responsible for safety documentation. It is important to know something of the history of a business to understand how it functions today. According to Kaplan (1994), "In identifying marginal space as both a site of repression and resistance, location becomes historicized and theoretically viable—a space of future possibilities as well as the nuanced articulation of the past" (p. 143). AM Steel is a good ol' boy, steel and sweat, man's world. Even today, this predominately blue-collar world still views woman as the inferior employee. I have had many men object to my position, as they believe my paychecks would be better served for a workingman's family. They tell me "get married or starve, but do not take the food from a family's mouth." The dominant opinion is that women are trying to take away jobs from men (of course, the only ones trying to support themselves and their respective families). While this is completely *old school* and oppressively irrational, it is still widespread in the industry. The opinion of the majority is that women do not belong in this (or any) workplace. Women are deemed too lazy and emotional as well as lacking the intelligence and strength required to carry out steel mill functions. The men who hold these sexist attitudes bond together, regardless of race, to marginalize women's collective role and voice in the steel industry. My predecessors have made significant changes for women in the steel industry, but they have helped sustain stereotypes as well. Because of their generation, these women still seem caught up in some of the sexist attitudes ingrained in their politics of location. In their defense, however, they hired into a place that was structured for men. Their employment was tantamount to putting a tampon machine in Alfalfa and Spanky's "Women-Haters" Clubhouse. The men were born anywhere from 1900 to 1950, and they were just not used to women in industry. The challenge for any woman hired into the mill between 1968 and 1977 was to be recognized as a competent and valuable co-worker. The error that some of these women made was encouraging and confirming, through their own actions, some of the patriarchal attitudes men had about women. For example, a lot of these women expected their male co-workers to do the *hard work* for them. It was this failure "to present themselves to themselves and others as complex human beings, and thereby to contest the bombardment of negative, degrading stereotypes put forward by White supremacist ideologies" that was the source of their adversity (West, 1990, 261). Then came the new generation of steelworkers hiring in from 1994 to the present. This resurgence in hiring gave way to educated women and minorities, born between 1968 and 1980, who had never lived through segregation and who were unaware that women were *supposed* to stay at home. While there are currently only three people in my department with baccalaureate degrees (a 30-something Black male, a 30-something white female and myself), ironically we are still viewed as the minorities and intellectually and physically incapable of performing our jobs because of our age, gender and/or race.

I was told to report to the plant at 6:00 on a Monday morning. Sure, I had seen 6 a.m. before (on my way home from partying), but to be awake, cognizant and presentable, this was another matter entirely. I arrived at the plant and parked in the Training Center parking lot where my new boss would meet me so I could follow him to my new office. (I didn't report directly to my office because I would have never found it in a place this size.) I was about 15 minutes early, so I had a bit of time to wait for him. It was early October, and the sky was still completely black. The only light came from either the few entranceway fixtures at brick buildings that lined the street or from a large outdoor overhead crane. I felt like I had stepped through some Narnian closet door into a different world altogether. For the first time I felt I might understand something about my father, and I felt more connected to Carl Sandburg's poetry than people who don't work in this place could ever feel. It was chilly out, and just as I lit a cigarette, to add to the romance and despair of the situation, it began to rain. I rolled up my window, cracking it slightly to let a little of the smoke escape, which was fine with me, because honestly the place was a little creepy. I watched as the (flood) gates opened and *Steelworkers* started trudging through the gates. In my head I heard someone reading *On the Way* by Carl Sandburg (p. 28):

Little one, you have been buzzing in the books, Flittering in the newspapers and drinking beer with lawyers, And amid the educated men of the clubs you have been getting an earful of speech from trained tongues.Take an earful from me once, go with me on a hike Along the sand stretches on the great inland sea . . .

At 6 a.m. sharp, my supervisor, Frank, pulled up. He got out of the car long enough to introduce himself and to tell me to follow him. I proceeded the couple of miles to my office down the pothole and scrap-infested roads and finally pulled up at two trailers attached to a warehouse. I felt like I was in a scene from *Mad Max: Beyond the Thunderdome*, only this version lacked Mel and Tina and the ultra-cool outfits.

The rain was clearing, but the air was heavy with one of the most horrific odors I have ever experienced. I later learned that it was pickle acid from the building adjacent to ours. I held my breath and followed him into the west trailer to see my new office and meet my new co-workers. I would share this building with my supervisor Frank, the production coordinator Mike, and two inventory clerks, Bettie and Carl. As soon as I walked in, I felt overdressed and too young to be working there. My Ralph Lauren trousers were a far cry from the old jeans and the traditional mill "greens" that my co-workers were donning, and I was the only person in this building without a salt and pepper 'do. Frank was a married white male with a boyish gait. Mike was a married (divorced once, I found out later) white male. Instead of a mere, proper hello he said, "Oh, a Polish girl. My name ends in –ek which signifies royalty and yours ends in –ski, and that means commoner." I smiled like an idiot while chewing my tongue. In my head, I was cursing him and his mother for raising such a you-know-what. Carl was a married white male. He was polite and had a heavy accent and told me he was Macedonian, probably so I would not ask, and I told him, loud enough for Mike to hear, that I was Lithuanian, not Polish. Bettie was an unmarried (divorced) black female. She had an unmistakable confidence about her and a welcoming tone in her voice. I was grateful for her presence. I have always thought myself quite skilled at reading people, so I did a quick inventory:

- Frank—nervous; high-strung; new to the area
- Mike—arrogant; wants Frank's job; more than happy to boss me around
- Carl—bossy; knowledgeable; feels Eastern European connection with me
- Bettie—the *real*, unacknowledged boss; knows more about this area than the other three

I was pretty much on target with all of them. I will find it eternally, yet karmically, interesting that usually the first things we notice about others are the things we like/dislike about ourselves. It was also quickly apparent that the gender division of labor was far from equal. After the introductions, Frank showed me to my office and excused himself with the promise of a quick return. I thought I might be in the middle of a nightmare. It was a faux-wood paneled box with a dirty linoleum floor yellowed from time and grime, but not sunlight, as there was no window. The room was dimly lit (one of the fluorescent bulbs was out and the other humming). It smelled like mold and stale coffee, and there were sticky traps to catch mice and/or other rodents in every corner. I was mortified and afraid to sit down for fear of getting dirty (which you do every day). Frank returned with a pile of disorganized papers (sticky, crumpled, and dirty), smiled at me, and told me to get to work. Huh? What? The safety documents that lay in front of me might as well have been written in Swahili. I decided to go to Bettie for help. Fortunately, she was already walking my way to save me. She told me to get a cup of coffee or have a smoke and we would "figure this stuff out together." I quickly excused myself to the bathroom to freak out. The door was broken, and I had to hit it hard with my hip to get it to shut (I still, nearly eight years later, have to do this and have the permanent bruise to prove it). I just wanted to be alone with my thoughts, but I was not alone. I heard a trickling kind of sound, and that is when I first realized that it rains indoors in this place long after it has stopped raining outside. I thought to myself, "No wonder there are hardly any women out here in Hades."

"It's nice to be liked, but better by far to get paid." (Liz Phair)

Gender is a major player in the steel industry. As an example I will offer a story from my first week on the job. I was twenty-two years old, blonde, white, and female. Honestly, this was such a big deal that they could have charged admission just to see me. Sharing a trailer with three middle-aged white men (Frank, Mike and Carl) and a middle-aged Black woman (Bettie), I immediately gravitated toward Bettie because of my desire to be accepted by women and my higher trust/comfort level around my own gender. She is a year younger than my mother, and her children are the same ages as my brother and me. She took me under her wing. In the time I have known her she has become invaluable to me. For reasons which are too many to name, I can say that she is a saint and one of the strongest people I know. She retired last September (something for which I have yet to forgive her) and this place (including myself) is just not the same without her. She is family to me, the kind to like as well as love. It was a normal first week, learning the basics, but then I got a separate set of rules concerning my co-workers from Bettie, including not to go drinking with, share personal information with, or date or sleep with anyone who works for the company. This list was much more detailed and animated, but I do not wish to kill a tree in order to articulate accurately her entire lecture. This discussion was strangely interesting to me, but I appreciated the *heads up* and instantly liked Bettie for her attempt to school me on AM Steel survival tactics. I knew she would be my go-to on any question that required discretion, my confidante so to speak. I quickly understood why she did me this service. Our department had over two hundred people who worked *on the floor* in more manual labor, operational capacities. They were the first who came to view the sideshow attraction free of charge, as well as the first to attack. During the course of the week they made their way in, one after another. Some would speak to me and some would not. Bettie would *shoosh* most of them out like children. For the repeat offenders, she would throw out classics like, "You got shoes older than her. Get on outta here." The common theme was that the majority of them kept calling me Lily. Before I left work on Thursday, I approached Bettie on the subject. "What gives with the 'Lily' thing?" I asked her. She responded, "Lily White, baby." She proceeded to inform me of why I *really* ended up in this department. It seems that many of the women of the floor were vying for my job, but these particular women were less than decent to Bettie, so she told the boss to get a *Lily White* to fill the position. She told me that I should not take it personally, but that she could not have been happier to see a thin, young, blond, white girl walk in that first day. I was stunned and offended. Looking back, I cannot believe I was so naïve. Since I have always lived by my favorite quote by Fran Lebowitz, "Being offended is that natural consequence of leaving one's home," I decided that I was going to use this sexist and racist nickname to my advantage. The next morning was my first weekly departmental safety meeting to which there is mandatory attendance for all department employees so everyone was there. One of the middle-aged Black men approached me, he leaned in with outstretched hand and introduced himself, "Simon. Simon Jefferson." Leaning in as well, and with a handshake, I responded, "Lily. Lily White. Nice to meet you." The room fell silent, but he grinned and still shaking my hand, he said, "You'll do fine out here, kid." Thus was the beginning of my experience as the *other*. The insolence or courage of my response (each person saw it differently) was my first step in cross-dressing in that it was an unexpected riposte from a female and therefore deemed mannish. My *call me what you want, but I am here to stay* attitude won respect from most of the employees in the department. While I had identified myself as the *other*, I had introduced myself in the same tone and manner as my co-worker had introduced himself to me. Although we did not share the same age, race, or gender, at that moment we understood each other. We were different, but we were steelworkers.

This situation was essentially a test. Was I a steelworker or not? Could I take the insult of being called Lily White? The answer was yes, so one point for me. Was I gutsy enough to say something about, it or would I just keep my mouth shut? I said something about it, so another point for me. For a woman, being a steelworker, or assuming any blue collar, male-dominated position, means she must be able to cross-dress when it comes to gender. She must be perceived by her co-workers as *tough enough* to handle the place. Blumstein (1991) maintains, "interpersonal competence is an aggregation of skills that allow one actor to prevail over another in defining the situation, that is, in assuring the working consensus captures a reality that supports his or her goals and desires" (p. 301). The Lily White situation was the first of many trials. A woman's speech and dress are the details about which she must be most cognizant. My co-workers would use profanity around me for shock value and to see whether or not I would report their behavior to management *like a typical woman*. I ignored their behavior as if they had not used foul language at all, and eventually they got tired of using it around me. Over the years my speech has changed somewhat. From time to time I do employ *mill talk* for added emphasis. I do, however, tailor my language to the receiver in a conversation, but as I deal with mostly Union and lower management it is not beyond me, and it is actually sometimes necessary, to *drop the f-bomb*. The general patriarchal rule concerning speech in the steel industry is do as I say not as I do. While the use of mild or occasional profanity is deemed acceptable, too much of it makes you un-ladylike and essentially leaves the door open for male co-workers to use sexual innuendo when speaking to a woman. Goffman (1959) suggests "that the performer must act with expressive responsibility, since many minor, inadvertent acts happen to be well designed to convey impressions inappropriate at the time" (p. 208). Matter-of-fact speech and sarcasm are a woman's best language choices in this industry. They are not only acceptable, but deemed arrogant as well. While I realize that arrogant speech in a normal setting would be considered highly inappropriate, here it is revered. I tried to model the way Bettie would speak. I watched how they feared and disliked Bettie. She made everyone nervous because she knew more about our area than anyone else did—union or management alike. Women envied or detested her, and men would hit on her relentlessly. I always found their advances interesting. I would overhear a co-worker talking about all the b!#$%es in the department and then walk right into Bettie and Nikola's office and hit on her. Was it a real attraction, a jealousy, or maybe a way of keeping her in her place as female? Since she had strict rules about dating co-workers, which stemmed from mistakes she had made in the workplace in her twenties, she refused every advance. She would give each and one of them a simple *no* the first few times and then she would resort to the crass, but nonetheless effective, "You can't do anything to me that hasn't been done before and done well." If that did not *do the job* she would yell my name at the top of her lungs for me to handle the situation. It became a sort of joke, but I would simply *shoosh* these men out for her—the same way she had done for me my first few weeks on the job. To this day, Mike calls me Mini-Bettie, a reference to the movie *Austin Powers*.

My clothing choice has also changed from business casual to more androgynous. When I first hired in I was always well dressed, nothing tight or too feminine and never a skirt, but I did not look like a steelworker. I had more men ask me out on dates my first month working for AM Steel than I have in my entire life. I guess I just never expected someone my father's age to be interested in me—naïve once again. The turning point for me regarding my clothing choices was when I found out that the first agenda item in the morning production meeting was *What is Ami wearing?* It had never occurred to me that not looking like *one of the guys* could create such a stir. I never made a big deal about this situation. I casually commented on it to Frank one afternoon, just so he would know that I knew what was going on. He turned red, and that was the last I ever heard of it. From my source on the subject, it was Frank being questioned, though, rather than participating. He knew how serious the legal implications associated with this information were if they traveled the grapevine back to me, and that is probably why the topic died. After this, I started to change my dress to avoid similar future scenarios. From then on, and still today, I wear jeans with a hole in the knee, an old boyfriend's t-shirt that is one step away from becoming a bathroom rag, and my grungy old metatarsal boots. As far as make-up is concerned—under-eye concealer and I am done—which is a big stretch for a girly-girl like me. My personal and social identity have learned to co-exist. According to Coover & Murphy (2000), "personal identities are based on idiosyncratic life experiences that make each individual distinctly different from all others. Social identities refer to identities that categorize the individual as a group member" (p. 129). My dress had to change because of female co-worker reactions as well. Because most of my day is spent in my office, I could dress more professionally than someone working in the warehouse, for instance. A majority of my female co-workers treated me like I was prissy and thought myself better than them. It was not until I started *dressing down* that their attitudes about me began to change. As I am the only white female in my department, race is still an issue, but only for a small number of these women. Strangely enough, race seems to be inconsequential to male co-workers. Changing one's dress and self-monitoring one's speech alone do not protect a woman in such an environment. The men in my department, aside from new hires, know better than to treat me with any sort of disrespect to my face, but this is a big place, and we are constantly dealing with people from other departments. I have learned to take heed of my mother's words to *choose your battles wisely*. I have come close to the breaking point many times, but 1) I like to eat, so un-

employment would not suit me, and 2) I find it a great disservice to my female co-workers when one of *us* acts crazy (which is what is expected of us).
At least once a week (and I promise my nose is not growing as I type these
words), I have the following situation happen to me, so I will therefore not
single out any one of the offenders by name. A male employee, possibly in
the area to perform maintenance on a piece of our equipment, will enter my
trailer. If I am the first person he sees, he will either immediately walk away
(without speaking a mere *Hey, how ya doin'?*) to look for a man; or he will
ask me a question, look at my chest while I am answering and then walk
away, find a man (even if it is obviously the janitor who does not know a thing
about this area) and ask him the same question. Every time this happens, I
want to put my hands around his throat and say, "Never in life ask me a question again. And if you ever look anywhere but at my face when speaking with
me, I'll poke yer f-in' eyes out." I get warm fuzzy feelings just imagining myself saying this. It would be my luck, however, that such a stand would make
the man in question have a stroke right in front of me. I would feel partially
responsible and worry that irreparable damage had been done in the karma
department. I hold on to the polite person's notion that he will get his come-
uppance. It is just hard to stomach, in this day and age, that someone would
automatically think me stupid because I am female. I am no different than
him—I am a *Steelworker,* and I think that should count for something. But
*outsiders* do not know me, and to them I do not look like a *Steelworker* or
someone with answers but rather someone to make their coffee. What does a
*Steelworker* look like? It is a mystery to me. We have got it all: short, tall,
skinny, overweight, black, white, Hispanic, Asian, gay, lesbian, bisexual,
trans-gendered, shelter volunteers, junkies, Bible beaters, megalomaniacs,
kleptomaniacs, 18 year-olds and 67 year-olds. So I ask again: what does a
*Steelworker* look like? As in *The Mayor of Gary* with workers possessing
"bunches of specialized muscles around their shoulder blades hard as pig
iron, muscles of their forearms were sheet steel, and they looked to me like
men who had been somewhere" (Sandburg, p. 161). Where is the common
link? It is when we pass through those gates off Virginia, Broadway, or
Buchanan—then we are all *Steelworkers.* I have had minor cross-dressing set-
backs, however. There is one day that I will never forget; it was New Year's
Eve, 1998. I was sitting in my office working on a project and Carl and our
area's union griever, Jeff, were in the other office. I realized I needed a file
out of my bottom left desk drawer, so I opened it. Now, I am no 'fraidy cat,
but when I opened that drawer and a little brown mouse was high-tailing it
across the tops of my files, I thought I saw a bright light calling me home. I
let out a big *wah-hoo* and high-tailed it into the other office. I was sweating
and shrieking and inarticulately trying to describe what just happened. Carl

and Jeff, both laughing, were finally able to ascertain my problem. Jeff went to search my office and determined that I had scared the hell out of the little fur ball and that I could safely re-enter my office. This did nothing to assuage my fears, but I had work to do. I put rubber bands around the bottoms of my jeans so the little intruder could not run up my pant leg. While I am not the first person (male or female) to have an adverse reaction to a rodent, Jeff took this as a sign of female vulnerability. While he had only casually *tried* to flirt with me up until this point, he now felt like my knight in shining hardhat and assumed that I would want to repay the debt. He began (relentlessly) to ask me to go out with him. Nothing so normal as dinner and a movie but a six-pack and a hotel. Ooh la la, très chic! Was it his attractive come-on or the fact that he has a wife and three kids that made me say no? Whatever it was, he was not pleased and decided to make it his personal *raison d'être* to try to make me as miserable as possible. While this did work, I never let onto him how much his behavior got to me. While I will not claim that being *tortured* on a daily basis is easy, I will say that my mere two years of *Steel Mill Experience* were all I needed to handle this situation. Coover & Murphy (2000) claim "Individuals who have more complex self-concepts are both able to think of themselves in different ways and are oriented toward a greater number of situations in their self-representations" (p. 131). I still work with him. After three years of my slamming doors and under-the-breath curses, he now speaks to me again.

This place makes me think that everything comes back to gender. Of course, there are other factors of race, age, sexuality, etc. Gender, though, seems to be the center of the vortex. Up until this point, I have made it seem like all the men I work with are pigs. This is unfair and untrue. I work with some exceptional and good-hearted people. As for the rest of them, and while I am not defending any of their behaviors, I believe that a lot of it has to do with age. When I hired in there was only one other person in my department in his twenties, Randy. He is two years my senior, and we had much in common. We instantly became friends and eventually became so close that we, and our friends, would take an annual trip to Hilton Head, South Carolina, together. To our co-workers, however, this meant that we were sleeping together. I do not know if it was their generations' lack of inter-departmental gossip, but Randy and I were a hot topic until he finally left the area to work in the Sales department. It felt like a junior high school dance. Boys and girls on opposite sides and only the *fast* girls would dance. I am well aware that I used the sexist term *fast*. I merely wanted to illustrate the extent to which gender inequality and stereotypes are deeply engrained in their heads. Perhaps the worst culprit was Mike, our coordinator. Wednesday was Mike's hangover day. Every Wednesday our trailer reeked of vodka and sarcasm. It was so apparent that if you stood too close, you would feel tipsy. One such day, Randy and I were hiding out in his office, to avoid the wrath and breath of Mike, under the pretext of employee training issues. The door was not locked, but we did have it closed. There was a small square window on the top of this door from which you could see passers-by. As we were chatting, we heard the familiar creak from the stairs that leads to the platform from which all the east trailer doors are accessed. No one passed by the window, however, and no one entered the office door located just before Randy's door. Now we were both well aware that Mike kept a vigil over everything the two of us did (the inherent curse of middle management), but he had never stooped to the level of eavesdropping (or so we thought). When no one passed by the door, however, we knew that someone was up to no good. Randy and I kept talking, only gesturing this knowledge and what we might do to find out who was crouching by the door. We both rose from our chairs as quietly as humanly possible and crept to the office door. Randy flung it open, as hard as you can fling open a trailer door, which is not difficult because they shut hard but open something like Styrofoam). Since the door opened outward and swung to the right, it was not a wise decision for Mike to be squatting on this side of the door. The red mark on the side of his face was barely noticeable by the end of the day, but the scarlet letter for Peeping Tom would forever stick. After his initial embarrassment, which unfortunately does not last in the truly wicked, he made sure that Randy and I had limited contact.

"Anyone who has begun to think places some portion of the world in jeopardy." (John Dewey)

Why gender? Why is this the main topic? Why do we have to be on different sides of the fence? Can't we all just get along? Why do stereotypes persist? Why do I remain in this atmosphere? Aside from the few comical moments in my work history, there have been some extremely difficult, insulting, and dehumanizing experiences. So, I repeat, why do I remain here? It is because this place feels like home to me. How does the saying go . . . You can't pick your family? That is how I feel about AM Steel. They are family, in sickness and in health, and I think my presence alone has changed the course for myself as well as some of my co-workers. At the pub the other night, I heard a lovely line in a song from a local Irish band: "Close your eyes and the story-line must be changed." What this says to me is that the simplest action can result in someone's life, opinion, and even identity shifting and transforming. Have these negative situations not helped to make me a better person? Did not the mere acquaintance of Frank, Mike, Carl, and Bettie forever change my life?

These experiences, and so many others, taught me to be aware of my politics of representation. I must create an identity conducive to my surroundings in order to function productively with and among my co-workers and must sustain this identity with constant and consistent reinforcing behaviors. The sustaining of identity, in my case, has been elusive at times, but always present. I can see it in the way that my co-workers treat me now as opposed to when I was *fresh meat*. Earlier I claimed that the malleability of one's identity was akin to Darwin's survival of the fittest. But is it not more complex than that? Does not the true essence lie in one's self-concept in regard to her identity? Must one not be comfortable with the identity she is communicating/ projecting/performing in relation to her politics of location? Coover & Murphy (2000) argued that "Whether motivated to maintain optimal distinctiveness or to achieve a positive social identity, the multifaceted self adapts to the cultural norms and situational constraints of any social interaction" (p. 129). If this is true, then what does my attempt to gender cross-dress at work say about my identity as a whole? Am I sacrificing my true self, my personal identity? Or am I simply evolving and being open to the *other*? Am I allowing hegemonic powers to force me into the role of gender cross-dressing and essentially denying my personal identity? I do not think so—the shift was easy and virtually effortless—it was already a part of me—uncharted territory.) Kaplan (1994) argued that the most constructive use of a politics of location, with regard to a feminist perspective, is "when it is used to deconstruct any dominant hierarchy or hegemonic use of the term gender" (p. 139). Am I setting all women, including myself, back? Cooley (183) maintains "the thing that moves us to pride or shame is not the mere mechanical reflection of ourselves, but an imputed sentiment, the imagined effect of this reflection upon another's mind" (p. 183). I really believe that I am being open to the *other* and as the *other,* allowing the dominant forces to get a glimpse of industry's inevitable paradigm shift into a more diverse workforce. I am a giver. You would not *go hatin'* on a cat for eating a bug, so why do the same to yourself for possibly helping others, by example, on how to be open to the *other?* As my late, great co-worker, Annie Huria, used to say, "Don't piss on my shoe and tell me it's raining." Blumstein's (1991) concept of ossification suggests that when we regularly perform an identity we *become* this person whom we have been performing (p. 298). That only suggests that prior to this point I was not whole. Life is a circle of ever-changing and intertwining events. While gender cross-dressing may have started for me as a means of survival, in retrospect, now I see the larger picture where I truly have just come to know a different part of myself, something previously undiscovered, and have been able to share that with others. We *all* have *miles to go before we sleep*, so why not begin by learning more about ourselves and leading such endeavors as these by breaking dehumanizing stereotypes and divisions through open and sharing examples of embracing each others' differences. First and foremost, we are all human beings, and I believe the most important thing we can do, for ourselves and for others, is to affect the quality of the day. "She who obtains has little. She who scatters has much" — Lao-Tzo.

## REFERENCES

Blumstein, P. (1991). The production of selves in personal relationships. In J. Howard & P. Callero (Eds.) *The self-society dynamic* (pp. 305–322). New York: Cambridge University Press.

Cooley, C. H. (1983). *Human nature and the social order*. New Brunswick, NJ: Transaction Publishers.

Coover, G. E., & Murphy, S. T. (2000, January). The communicated self: Exploring the interaction between self and social context. *Human Communication*, 6, 125–147.

Goffman, E. (1959). *The presentation of self in everyday life*. New York: Doubleday.

Kaplan, C. (1994). The politics of location as transnational feminist practice. In I. Grewal & C. Kaplan (Eds.), *Scattered hegemonies: Postmodernity and transnational feminist practices* (pp. 137–152). Minneapolis, MN: University of Minnesota Press.

Neumann, M. (1996). Collecting ourselves at the end of the century. In C. Ellis & A. P. Bochner (Eds.), *Composing autoethnography: Alternative forms of qualitative writing* (pp. 172–198). Walnut Creek, CA: AltaMira Press.

Sandburg, C. (1970). *The complete poems of Carl Sandburg*. New York: Harcourt Brace & Company.

West, C. (1990). The new cultural politics of difference. In S. During (Ed.), *The cultural studies reader* (2nd ed.) (pp. 256–267). New York: Routledge

*Ami and Her Brother, Kristopher*

## Chapter Eight

# William Boggs: What My Father Taught Me

## Script Six: June Bug's House and Photographs and Memories

*When I was informed that one of my students was a conservative Evangelical Christian minister, I was concerned. My previous experiences had dictated that with such a student, his belief in God would take over my classroom and intimidate all present. Instead, I was met with a pleasant surprise. Bill Boggs was an open-minded individual with whom I shared a similar past—a lifetime of conflict initiated by our fathers. Bill's master narrative is about growing up with an abusive father and coming to understand the havoc this history wreaked on his life. Bill's work is a form of survival, not resolution. By naming the history, he sets himself free.*

### JUNE BUG'S HOUSE

I like the Andy Griffith Show. I've always liked it. I'm especially drawn to the poignant moments where kind, wise, funny, and gentle Andy sits on the edge of young Opie's bed, and, in a spurt of slow Southern direction, guides the young man through the major issues of life. Is it the father-son interaction that grabs me? Maybe the Southern setting that reminds me of my early years in eastern Kentucky? No, more likely it's the depiction of some fatherly ideal, some model or example that I've always longed for. Something I missed, something that has left me incomplete, maybe even defective.

There were no edge-of-my-bed wisdom dispersals from my father. Nothing resembling a kind, wise, and gentle man was ever of a part of my formative years. Compared to the fictional Andy Taylor, I lived with an increasingly hostile monster for the first eight years of my life. I remember being eight years old.

And I remember June Bug's house.

It should have been a scary night—especially for an eight-year-old boy. Much of it seemed like a blur. The end was clear . . . my mother frantically trying to herd my brother, sister, and me out of our harm's-way house and over to June Bug's in the middle of the night. June Bug Hern was my friend who lived next door with his parents. The Herns still live there today.

I don't remember the events leading up to that night. I just remember getting awakened in the middle of the night by a crazy but typical commotion. My father, William Norman Boggs, Sr., came home in a monstrous, drunken rage. As usual, he was terrorizing my mother, Joan. She was trying hard to stay out of his way. He was just getting madder. I sneaked into the living room to get a look at the two adults I loved most in the world locked in mortal combat.

And yet it all seemed normal to me. Dad's drunk and mad at my mom; she's trying to protect herself and us—just another day at 3106 Charles Street in Ashland, Kentucky, 1964.

Dad's frustration at not getting a clear crack at my mom sent him to a whole new level of destruction.

CRASH!

The refrigerator became his surrogate wife as he grabbed the top of it and sent it slamming into the kitchen floor. As he moved into the living room, the television was next in his path. I backed down the hall trying to stay out of sight. He hadn't torn into me or Jimmy or Cindy so far in these rages, but I didn't want to press my luck. There was what sounded to me like an explosion. How did he bash in the picture tube? Did he use his foot . . . or, wait; was that a pistol in his hand? I don't know. Why wasn't I scared? Numbness was my friend. Detachment was my salvation.

By now, my mother was scrambling to rush us out the back door and over to the Herns. She called the police from there. They took Bill Boggs away that evening. I was worried about going outside in my pajamas.

This was just another event in my absurd world, in the school of manhood. What did I learn that night? There were the obvious lessons . . . that violence is acceptable, that wives are suitable targets, that refrigerators, televisions, and furniture will do if a wife is out of range, and that alcohol is a suitable lubricant for the family dynamic.

My world changed after that night. My mother had had enough of the violence, the adultery, and the chaos. She filed for divorce, an act of raw courage as an uneducated woman in the early 1960s, in the face of no visible means of support beyond what the court ordered of my father. Had she known then that after the court divorce proceedings, that very day, my father would disappear, completely ignoring his legal and moral responsibility to provide for his children, well, she would have put up with the abuse.

As my father prepared to desert his post, as he packed up whatever he packed up to make his escape from all responsibility to his children, I doubt he realized *all* he was tossing in with his argyle socks and Old Spice after shave.

Into that bag he was cramming my self-worth and my potential for intimate relationships. I wonder if he had to sit on his suitcase to get it closed because it was jammed so full with my ability to love and to trust; he took them away, too. They were mine; he took them. Surely his luggage was overloaded. Did he realize he had already removed my ability to feel, leaving me with a numbness that I would learn to use as a shield, a numbness that would lull me toward devastation and shove me toward repeating his mistakes?

At this point the lesson that I was abandon-able and worthless, that even people close to me would leave me alone, began to take shape. As I look back, I think I'm thankful the numbness kept the pain of this lesson away from my fragile eight-year-old heart.

What is a man? Surely not what I've seen.

## PHOTOGRAPHS AND MEMORIES

My father died in March 1976, age 49, the same age I am now, from cirrhosis of the liver. Justice, I guess. After the divorce I never saw him again alive. There was no contact whatsoever, though we tried to find him. I went to his funeral to satisfy my own curiosity. I wanted to look at the man, to see his face. Yet even after he was dead, the lessons my father taught me continued. Let me tell you another one.

There's a whole industry now focused on preserving memories. My wife has attended and hosted dozens of scrapbooking parties, sought out scrapbooking stores, given scrapbooking gifts, bought more than a few scrapbooking supplies, and offered scrapbooking advice to the less-creative memory-retaining novices around. She has even produced several very nice scrapbooks, volumes that effectively capture little visual moments of our lives to prod us to remember good times. I like to look at them.

By living in proximity to this effective memory preservation, I've learned all about legacy inks and acid-free paper and cute little stickers and special scissors that cut a squiggly pattern that maybe someone out there thinks is attractive. I've also learned well that all that stuff is expensive.

*But I already knew that photographs and memories could carry a price.*

Less than two years after my father's funeral, I was married, out of the Marines, and back in Indiana. Bill Boggs Senior had now assumed a permanent place in my thoughts. I got married right after his funeral, and a year later my wife had our baby daughter. I was now a father myself and scared to death, often prone to worrying I would repeat my father's mistakes.

We got a call from our all-but-forgotten Florida attorney. He told me that my father's common-law wife had died and my father's house was now ours.

I was now entitled to anything belonging to my father. Again my curiosity was piqued. As I prepared to go, I found myself getting nervously excited. I was going to get to connect in some way to my lost father, to enter his world, to touch his things, to see how he lived. After struggling with forgiving him, a requirement of my new Christian faith, I had prayed that God would let me find my father, to confront him for his behavior and ask him why. Evidently, here was my answer.

I drove to Florida. My thoughts raced as I designed and played out scenario after scenario of what I would find. Tears often came to my eyes as I let myself remember the school pictures I always sent to his mother to give to him.

Pictures were little symbols of care, of love, of concern. Would I find those pictures among my father's things? Would I find anything that might suggest that despite his many problems he *did* care about me? Would I find proof that I was lovable, that my father loved me?

It had become increasingly inconceivable to me that a father could do what my father had done. As the daddy of an especially adorable little baby girl myself, I could not imagine just walking away one day, never seeing her, never watching her grow up, never knowing what kind of person she would become. No, it wasn't possible for a *human* father to do that, and now I would find evidence. I would *prove* my father did love me. I would finally see that I did have value. If I could just find *one* picture. . . .

I met my lawyer and the unknown stepmother's family lawyer at the house. My heart was trying to loose its bodily bounds, pounding like a gavel, nearly loud enough, I was sure, for the lawyers to hear, making them feel at home. At least someone did. What would I find? A better question was why had I let myself get so worked up with unsubstantiated hope for this? I was on a wild treasure hunt with life-or-death implications. Yes, significance for me might be found in that little Clearwater, Florida, house. If my father loved me, then I would not be unlovable and abandon-able after all, and I could turn my not-so-good ship, Crippled Emotions, around. I stood ready to embrace my father that day, to move from act-of-the-will forgiveness to rich, heartfelt, relationship-restoring forgiveness.

*I entered the world of William Norman Boggs Senior as I crossed the doorstep into the living room.*

It was a dreary little place. Dark. And disturbingly cold, not from the temperature but emotionally somehow. Appropriate, I guess. The furnishings were cheap and ragged with general housekeeping to match. I wasn't deterred

as I walked into something like Bill Boggs' life for the first time in my memory. My emotions were roaring up and down, all over the place, like the Or-
lando roller coasters not far away. As I moved from room to room I even felt
a little dizzy. *Excitement! Anticipation! Fear!* All engaged in combat, trying
to establish control, dominance of my emotions. The internal battle raged.

It didn't take long to examine the tiny five-room house. I saved the master
bedroom for last, thinking that was the most likely location for the care-evi-
dence I sought.

My heart was pounding furiously now as I got inside the bedroom. I had to
steady myself. I was tingling all over. A quick search of the dresser drawers
produced the typical stuff. I was desperate to start tearing through the piles,
ready to dig like a madman.

Finally I found a box, the kind of cardboard "safe deposit" shoebox people
use to stash important papers, cufflinks, and other keepsakes. The *pictures?*
Was I finally going to see evidence that my father cared about me after all?

My hands shook as I sat on the bed with the box. I wanted everyone to
leave, but I said nothing. No one knew what I was thinking. I hadn't said a
word about this personal quest for significance. They had no idea what hinged
on the contents of that box in my heart. There was my father's Florida driver's license! The same face I had seen in the casket. His stuff *was* in this box.
I was a very sweaty hopeful now.

*Then, there they were!* Under some miscellaneous papers was a stack of
*pictures!* I frantically tossed aside the papers and began to look at the photographs.

It was an incredible blow. Nothing could have prepared me for what I was
about to see. None of the photos were of me, my brother, sister, or mother.
My father's treasure of memories consisted of dozens of homemade pornog-
raphy photos of himself with various women, one-on-one and in groups.

I was on the receiving end of another of his sick and cruel lessons. I barely
kept from throwing up. I was overwhelmingly repulsed by what I saw. Hor-
ribly embarrassed in front of the lawyers. Disgusted. The flood of feelings
nearly toppled me. Two giant tidal waves of emotion. . . one of hope, the other
despair, rammed into each other with incredible force. *Despair greatly over-
powered hope* as I crumbled into a heap of human mush.

In seconds, I had gone from positive feelings about my father to sickened
devastation. Had I found no pictures at all, I would have been disappointed
and moved on. Instead, finding this evidence of his twisted immorality
greatly deepened the hurt he had already inflicted by abandoning me. I hate
that I saw those images.

I had been willing to spin his abandonment of me into something I could
understand. . . that the alcoholism had led him to leave me, that he regretted

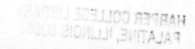

it and struggled for years about it. That he treasured the photos he had of me, that he knew of and was proud of my achievements. That my mother's family had described him with prejudice. That it was all a sad mistake for which he was sorry.

I hoped to find evidence that he had turned his life around. That he was living sober, attending AA, and going to church regularly. I *even* dared to hope I'd find some kind of written plan or diary containing his desire to find us and apologize (*I guess I've always had an overactive imagination, an adult child of an alcoholic trait, I'm told*).

What amazed me later was the elaborate detail I developed for my visit to the Bill Boggs theme park. That was the fiction I had prepared. . .all I needed to turn it into reality was a *picture* of me in that shoebox. Just one picture.

Years of buried pain charged to the surface. I faced a bitter, distorted reality. I started that day on my own course of self-destruction. I strapped on additional weight. The chasm between good and evil in my own heart widened.

Now I was convinced there was no good in my father, no good in me. Bill Boggs Senior was a narcissistic life-wrecking sperm donor with no redeeming value. Where did that leave me? With yet another horrible example of how to live as a man.

Scrap booking is designed to preserve good memories. That's the point. We archive the good memories to remember and pass on. So we won't forget. The bad memories need no such devices. They stay fresh all on their own.

# Afterword: Identity and Human Communication

Many of us who have immersed ourselves in the communication discipline hope to learn about the secrets and intricacies of the human communication process. From understanding the basic communication model of message from sender to receiver to exploring methodologies appropriate for the study of communication, little emphasis has been placed on the importance of identity in communication. Identity, I believe, holds the key to communication. Without an understanding of identity and how it molds our expression of self, we are doing a great injustice to the discipline.

With the scripts I have just presented, I have tried to show how identity is specifically tied to communication. The scripts represent individuals' lives and how they explain the processes of their lives—a phenomenology of identity. The process of eliciting these scripts was challenging and fascinating. Creating the opportunity for individuals to reveal themselves in a reflective script based on a primary narrative can only contribute to an ongoing dialogue about the nature of identity in the communication process. Simply put, when we understand others, we understand ourselves so much better, which leads to a more holistic examination of the discipline.

Many of the earliest theorists like the constructivists, the rules theorists, the systems' theorists, and the symbolic interactionists, sought to lasso communication by providing a context to illuminate theory. Not wishing to diminish these areas of the discipline, I am calling for a more holistic examination that invites intimate intrapersonal engagement between scriptwriters and their stories and reveals a unique sensibility. This process acknowledges the individuality of communication and does not encourage generalized findings. Such exploration can yield new insights into how each of us experiences and responds to new information, thus maximizing the opportunity for dialogue between scriptwriter and audience, and audience and other members of a community.

# References

Bebout, S. (1991). *To know from the inside out: an approach to the performance of the culturally familiar*. Dissertation, Southern Illinois University, Carbondale, Illinois.

Bochner, A. P., & Ellis, C. (Eds.). (1996). *Composing ethnography: Alternative forms of qualitative writing*. Walnut Creek, CA: Altamira Press.

Bochner, A. P., & Ellis, C. (Eds.). (2001). *Ethnographically speaking: Autoethnography, literature, and aesthetics*. Walnut Creek, CA: Altamira Press.

Bruner, E. (1986). Ethnography as narrative. In V. Turner & E. Bruner (Eds.), *The anthropology of experience*. Urbana: University of Illinois Press.

Carilli, T. (1990). *Healing through personal narratives*. Unpublished manuscript.

Carilli, T. (1998). Verbal promiscuity as healing art?: Writing the creative/performative personal narrative. In S. J. Dailey (Ed)., *The future of performance studies: Visions and revisions*. (pp. 232–236). Annandale, VA: National Communication Association Press.

Clifford, J., & Marcus, G. E. (Eds.). (1986). Writing culture: The poetics and politics of ethnography. Berkeley, CA: University of California Press.

Conquergood, D. (1985). Performing as a moral act: Ethical dimensions of the ethnography of performance. *Literature in Performance*, 5, 1–13.

Denzin, N. K. (2003). *Performance ethnography: Critical pedagogy and the politics of culture*. Thousand Oaks, CA: Sage Publications, Ltd.

Geertz, C. (1973). *Interpretation of cultures*. New York: Basic Books.

Geertz, C. (1983). *Local knowledge: Further essays in interpretive anthropology*. New York: Basic Books.

Langellier, K. M. (1989). Personal narratives: Perspectives on theory and research. *Text and Performance Quarterly*, 9, 243–276.

Langellier, K. M. (1998). Voiceless bodies, bodiless voices: The future of personal narrative performance. In S. J. Dailey (Ed)., *The future of performance studies: Visions and revisions*. (pp. 207–213). Annandale, VA: National Communication Association Press.

Langellier, K. M., & Peterson, E. E. (2004). *Storytelling in daily life*. Philadelphia: Temple University Press.

Lockford, L. (2004). Performing femininity: Rewriting gender identity. Lanham, MD: Altamira Press.

Marcus, G., & Fischer, M. (1986). *Anthropology as cultural critique*. Chicago: University of Chicago Press.

Montalbano-Phelps, L. (2004). *Taking narrative risk*. Lanham, MD: University Press of America.

Myeroff, B. (1980, March). Telling one's story. Center Magazine, 22–40.

Okely, J., & Callaway, H. (1992). *Anthropology & autobiography*. New York: Routledge.

Pelias, R. J. (1999). *Writing performance: Poeticizing the researcher's body*. Carbondale: Southern Illinois University Press.

Pelias, R. J. (2004). *A methodology of the heart: Evoking academic & daily life*. Lanham, MD: Altamira Press.

Pelias, R. J., & VanOosting, J. (1987). A paradigm for performance studies. *Quarterly Journal of Speech*, 73, 219–231.

Schechner, R. (1985). *Between theatre and anthropology*. Philadelphia: University of Pennsylvania Press.

Turner, V. (1986). *The anthropology of performance*. New York: PAJ Publications.

Turner, V. (1985). Performing ethnography. *The Drama Review*, 26, 33–48.

# About the Author

**Theresa Carilli**, Ph.D., Professor of Communication and Creative Arts, teaches at Purdue University Calumet. She has published two book of plays, *Familial Circles* (2001) and *Women As Lovers* (1996), co-edited two anthologies, *Women and the Media: Diverse Perspectives* (2005), and *Cultural Diversity and the U.S. Media* (1998). Carilli has guest edited a theater issue of *Voices in Italian Americana* and co-edited a special issue on women and the media for the *Global Media Journal.* She has one forthcoming book of short stories, *What You Do Know Could Kill You*. She has published numerous performance texts and articles that explore the connection between culture and the creative process.